BABYLON REVISITED

The Screenplay

Photo by Belle O'Hara

F. Scott Fitzgerald

BABYLON REVISITED

The Screenplay

With An Introduction by
BUDD SCHULBERG

Carroll & Graf Publishers, Inc.
New York

This edition published by arrangement with the Estate of Lester Cowan.

First Carroll & Graf edition 1993

Carroll & Graf Publishers, Inc.
260 Fifth Avenue
New York, NY 10001

Library of Congress Cataloging-in-Publication Data

Fitzgerald, F. Scott (Francis Scott), 1896–1940.
    Babylon revisited : the screenplay / with an introduction by
Budd Schulberg. — 1st Carroll & Graf ed.
        p.   cm.
    ISBN 0-88184-968-5 : $10.95
    I. Title.
PS3511.I9B315   1993
791.43′72—dc20   93-14013
                                                         CIP

Manufactured in the United States of America

Cover illustration: *To Beauty* (1922) by Otto Dix. Otto Dix Stiftung, Valduz.
Used with permission.

CONTENTS

INTRODUCTION
Budd Schulberg

I met Scott Fitzgerald in Hollywood, in 1939, when the golden boy of the literary twenties was desperate for movie work. Thousands of dollars a week could be made by "name" writers, and "by F. Scott Fitzgerald" had not lost all of its luster, even if he was now considered a fallen star who had reached his zenith with *The Great Gatsby*, and had faded fast in the thirties of Steinbeck, James T. Farrell, and Clifford Odets.

The Scott Fitzgerald I knew had made some money at MGM, working on an odd assortment of film scripts, but his track record as a screenwriter was negligible. Though he had received a "co-adapted by" credit for his work on *Three Comrades* (the film based on Erich Maria Remarque's novel), his producer Joe Mankiewicz had felt it necessary to rewrite Fitzgerald's script, a blow to Scott's pride and to his reputation at the studio. While writing books, or memorable short stories (like "Babylon Revisited"), may help you get a foot in the studio door, what you needed to get all the way in and stay in was a solid screen credit, especially on a hit movie. You could write all the *May Days* or *The Rich Boys* you wanted, but the tough boys who ran the studios wanted to know what you had done for them lately—i.e., your last assignment, your last "credit" up there on the screen.

After eighteen remunerative but professionally frustrating months at MGM, Fitzgerald had been cast out into that limbo for Hollywood writers euphemistically described as "between pictures." I still remember my astonishment, my sense of awe, the day my producer (Walter Wanger) called me in to tell me he thought I needed a collaborator on the Dartmouth Winter Carnival movie I was trying to put together, and that the collaborator he had chosen was F. Scott Fitzgerald, now temporarily rescued from limbo.

Not only had I studied *Gatsby* in college, but, by coincidence, had only recently reread *Tender Is the Night*, which is simply so exquisitely written it makes you want to cry.

There is no space to dwell on our "Winter Carnival" debacle here, indeed I used it as the spine for a novel called *The Disenchanted*, about a famous novelist of the twenties who comes a-cropper in the Hollywood thirties. Working to develop a coherent screenplay for a meretricious college romance became an ordeal when Wanger insisted on our flying east and then trekking north to the snow and ice of the actual Winter Carnival. The strain of the trip, and the pressure of the work he so badly needed but couldn't help resisting, proved too much for his frail nervous system. We drank together and sank together, and Scott was sent home in disgrace.

But the tempest that tossed us and might have driven us apart instead brought us together, and from the late winter of 1939 to the last time I saw Scott, when I dropped in to say good-bye to him before leaving for the East just three weeks before he died, we remained friends. Unlike Hemingway, who bullied me, Scott was unfailingly endearing. After blowing the Wanger assignment, his Hollywood stock had fallen even lower, while his literary reputation, his price on the New York publishers' market, was in disarray. The Modern Library refused to include *Tender* in its prestigious list of classics, his lifetime publishers were leery of advancing him money for the novel he wanted to write (his ambitious Hollywood novel, posthumously published as *The Last Tycoon*), and he was hard-pressed to support his wife Zelda in a sanitarium after her breakdown and to put his adored daughter Scottie through Vassar. Scott was living from hand to mouth, cranking out sad/funny Hollywood short stories for *Esquire*, and urging his Hollywood agent to find him another film-writing job that would keep him from going under.

How Scott managed to keep his sanity and his essentially sweet nature during these dark days in sunny California reflected a quality I admired as much as I did the body of his work. He was like a man who refused to be drowned even after going down three times. Somehow he would surface again and heroically tread water.

Another quality of Scott's was his interest in film-writing and film-making. A host of famous authors or playwrights had come west, putting their literary or dramatic works aside in order to get on that Hollywood payroll. Dorothy Parker, Dashiell Hammett, William Faulkner, Nathanael West, and William Saroyan were a handful of the beautiful and damned who hung out at the Garden of Allah and the backroom of Stanley Rose's Book Store. Most of them saved their best lines for sarcastic descriptions of the film world. The sharp teeth of dogs biting the hand that fed them. Dorothy Parker had a gift for that even though her much-abused husband, Alan Campbell, handled most of their screenwriting, as I learned firsthand when Ring Lardner, Jr., and I were working with them as "junior writers" on the original *A Star Is Born*.

Instead of rejecting screenwriting as a necessary evil, Fitzgerald went the other way and embraced it as a new art form, even while recognizing that it was an art frequently embarrassed by the "merchants" more comfortable with mediocrity in their efforts to satisfy the widest possible audience. Still, Fitzgerald saw screen classics being made by Irving Thalberg (his model for Monroe Stahr in *The Last Tycoon*), David Selznick, even my father B. P. Schulberg, (at Paramount) who made *Dr. Jekyll and Mr. Hyde, Crime and Punishment,* and *An American Tragedy.* Fitzgerald not only made it his business to go to the movies, he told me, but he'd then go home and outline their plots and sequence development.

In spite of his homework and his proven gifts, Fitzgerald's stock had virtually reached bottom by the spring of 1940. That's when an independent producer, Lester Cowan, something of a maverick, and a fast-talker, approached Fitzgerald with an offer to buy his short story *Babylon Revisited* for nine hundred dollars, with an additional five thousand dollars to write the screenplay. That was known as "peanuts" for an industry willing to pay flamboyant Ben Hecht five thousand a week, but Fitzgerald grabbed it—"a last life-line has been thrown me," he wrote Zelda in the sanitarium.

Fitzgerald's life and career seemed to stagger from irony to irony, and here was another one: "Babylon Revisited" in many ways reflected Fitzgerald's own experience and ordeal. It was perhaps the first (and one of his best) short-story attempts to come to grips with the effects of the Crash. The party was over. Overnight millionaires had jumped out of windows and flappers were no longer flashing their dimpled knees. Zelda's breakdown and Fitzgerald's struggle with alcohol and his fall from grace were now expressed in somber, introspective stories like "Babylon," in which a young, hard-drinking stockbroker who had a golden touch when the market was soaring loses his wife when he locks her out on a stormy night and she dies of pneumonia, leaving a contrite, shaken Charlie Wales with a nine-year-old daughter (she is eleven years old in the screenplay.) A bitter sister-in-law blames Charlie for her sister's death and is determined to raise the child (Honoria in the story and early screenplay drafts) on the grounds that Charlie is an unfit, irresponsible father. The tug-of-war between Charlie and sister-in-law Marion for possession of the appealing Honoria is the essential story of "Babylon Revisited." But the setting provides the theme: the contrast between the Paris of the twenties and the thirties, the mood change in Charlie who lived it up in the Ritz Bar in the years of the bull market and no tomorrows, and has now returned to Paris to win back his daughter and start a new life. A second chance. Here the reformed alcoholic "Charlie Wales" of 1931 and his embattled creator (nine years later) are as one. Fitzgerald's reasons for embracing Cowan's assignment are painfully clear. Like Wales, Fitzgerald has come a long way down from the golden boy of the twenties. Wales's wife is dead and Fitzgerald had lost Zelda to the twilight years in the sanitarium. In 1940 Fitzgerald was consumed with both guilt and concern for his daughter Scottie. His letters to her are some of his most moving as he lectures her about her education and her progress, worries about money for her and reveals a desperate sense of paternal responsibility, even to worrying what gown she should wear to a certain social event.

At last, Fitzgerald felt, he could pour himself into a work of his own, at last an opportunity to adapt his own published story as a film production that would give him—he boasted to Zelda—"some real status out here as a movie man and not a novelist." It was in this mood that he telephoned me on that May 26 to congratulate me on the birth of my first child, Victoria. In her honor, he said, he would now change the name of his child protagonist in the script from Honoria (a bow to his old Cote D'Azur hosts Gerald and Sara Murphy for *their* daughter) to the name of my daughter. Accordingly, in the screenplay to follow, the child has become "Victoria." "When she's old enough to understand, you can tell her that the little girl in the movie, who may be played by Shirley Temple, was named for her!" Scott enthused. That long-ago evening there wasn't the slightest hint of doubt in his voice. He felt surely on his way to a coveted film credit, establishing himself as "a movie man" after years of trying—a strange goal for the author who rivaled Ernest Hemingway as the most celebrated novelist of his time.

Into the fall, with death waiting to ambush him, Fitzgerald kept working, and dreaming of Hollywood acceptance. But Fitzgerald's heart would cease to beat on December 21, 1940, with his last screenplay still unproduced. Not yet satisfied with Fitzgerald's work, Lester Cowan hired the Epstein twins (*Casablanca*) to do a rewrite, which he sold to MGM for $100,000, under the title of Elliot Paul's novel, *The Last Time I Saw Paris.*

Somehow Cowan retained Fitzgerald's screenplay, and in the late forties asked me if I was interested in revising it. I begged off, just as John O'Hara and I had begged off at the suggestion that we collaborate on finishing the half-completed *The Last Tycoon*. While I felt that Fitzgerald's adaptation failed to do justice to his short story, there is something about his work, even if it's not his premium stuff, that is difficult and risky to tamper with.

Not long after, I discussed that problem with Irwin Shaw, whom Cowan had also approached, and who shared my hesitation to walk in Fitzgerald's footsteps, even along a path more narrow and bumpy than some of the high roads Fitzgerald had taken in his memorable and troubled career.

Going through a carton marked "other people's manuscripts" a year or so ago, I came across the long-forgotten screenplay and communicated with Professor Matthew Bruccoli, the Fitzgerald specialist, regarding its publication. He agreed with me that there was value in adding Fitzgerald's own adaptation of his classic short story to the Fitzgerald shelf. Hence, this new volume.

While it may be a minor addition to the collected works, it does represent one of Fitzgerald's last-gasp efforts at establishing a second career, and as such has historical literary value, as well as containing a host of uniquely Fitzgerald "touches." Character and staging descriptions display gifts that would not die, along with a feel for dialogue that at its best evokes his special quality. How well he knew how to set a mood, and when it works it is marvelously right.

We move this "lost" manuscript from the shelf to publication with the admission that the piece is flawed. Most authors who adapt their own literary work are stubbornly faithful to their original creations. Fitzgerald, perhaps because he had become so immersed in screen technique, takes enormous liberties with his story, retaining the principal characters, Charlie Wales, Honoria/Victoria, and Marion, but adding an elaborate and sometimes top-heavy plot of business machinations, involving new characters that are still two-dimensional and seem unable to break through the mechanics of the plot Fitzgerald has imposed on them. In his zeal to "make a movie" rather than attempt to retell his short story in cinematic form, he has stood it on its head by having Charlie Wales triumph heroically at the end, even to his knocking out the young thug who's sent by his former business partner (now enemy) to kill him for the million-dollar-insurance policy this "heavy" has taken out on Charlie's life. It's all pretty melodramatic, and it concludes with a happy, Hollywood ending, the unsympathetic sister-in-law thwarted and Charlie and Honoria/Victoria reunited, with Charlie's final line, "Aw, there's a lot to live for." Fade out.

The ending of the short story is haunting, Fitzgerald at his best, rather than the rock-'em-sock-'em bathos with which Scott chooses to end his movie. The short story had Charlie on the threshold of regaining Honoria, when two jazzy throwbacks to his twenties merrymaking past show up at the worst possible moment, convincing the unforgiving sister-in-law that despite his protestations, Charlie is still an unfit father for her sister's precious daughter. Charlie retreats to the Ritz Bar where the maître'd says, "I heard you lost a lot in the crash," and Charlie answers, "I did, but I lost everything I wanted in the boom."

The story tapers off into bleak despair, closing with, "He wasn't young anymore, with a lot of nice thoughts and dreams to have by himself. He was absolutely sure Helen [his dead wife] wouldn't have wanted him to be so alone."

Of course, Fitzgerald the movie man knew that was all very well, in fiction, but no way to say "Fade Out . . . The End" on the silver screen. So he flipped the coin from "Tails, you lose, Charlie" to "Heads, you win!"

To read the short story and then study this screenplay is to understand the terrible contortions of an artist driven to turn himself inside out and upside down in one last desperate reach for Hollywood status. Read in this perspective, *Babylon Revisited—The Screenplay* makes a telling contribution to the life's work of F. Scott Fitzgerald, a project he was still

hoping to see on the screen when death wrote its premature
Fade Out in the closing days of 1940.

Despite his theory that the novel would become passé,
replaced by the new art of the motion picture, Fitzgerald the
novelist lives, while Fitzgerald the movie man remains an
almost-forgotten footnote to literary history.

—Budd Schulberg
May 1993

SEQUENCE A

FADE IN:

1. LONG SHOT—ESTABLISHING PARIS—with the superimposed title:

PARIS, OCTOBER 1929

2. EXTERIOR. MEDIUM-PRICED APARTMENT BUILDING ON A NICE STREET

3. INTERIOR. FRONT HALL OF AN APARTMENT
—as it might be furnished by the American wife of a Frenchman making thirty-five hundred dollars a year—which sum would go twice as far in the Paris of those days.

The eleven-year-old son of the house is in the hall putting his books into his school bag. His name is Richard Petrie (pronounced "Reeshard" in French) and he is more French than American; his hair is dark and close cropped; he wears glasses and a black schoolboy's apron.

RICHARD
> *(calling offscene, rather impatient and surly)*
> Qu'est-ce que tu as, Victoria? [What's the matter with you, Victoria?] We'll be late for school.

15

VICTORIA'S VOICE
> *(offscene)*
>
> I'm coming.

4. INT. VICTORIA WALES'S BEDROOM

She is an attractive little American girl of eleven, excellently brought up and without any self-consciousness or airs. In this part of our story, a certain gravity and preoccupation overshadows natural high spirits. Some one dominant purpose is driving her.

For the rest she is simply dressed, her glance is level and straight, and her enunciation is clearcut and not slangy—the effect of having been (up to recently) under the charge of an English governess.

Her bedroom is small, spare, and neat. On the bureau reposes her school sack, and at the moment Victoria is swiftly and quietly removing the books from it. She puts them in a bureau drawer from which she takes several pairs of socks, some underwear, and handkerchiefs. These, with a toothbrush and comb, she puts into the book bag.

RICHARD'S VOICE
> *(impatiently—over shot)*
>
> Victoria! Vien!

Victoria works quickly. She is almost ready. On the bureau stands a china bank in the shape of a pig. She cracks it with a hairbrush, pours into her purse the one- and two-franc pieces it contains, and puts the broken pig into the drawer. Slinging the school bag from her shoulder, she starts out.

5. INT. THE HALL

Richard impatiently opens the front door as Victoria comes out of her bedroom.

> *DISSOLVE TO:*

6. EXT. OPEN COURT OF THE APARTMENT

The children cross toward the gate in the morning sun-light.

7. UNDER THE ARCH OF THE GATE

As they pass the concierge's (janitor's) door, the concierge's wife, a fat, cheerful, peasant woman, comes out.

CONCIERGE'S WIFE

Bon jour, Reeshard.

THE CHILDREN

Bon jour, Madame Restaud.

CONCIERGE'S WIFE

(to Victoria)

And the little American cousin!

She gives a flower to Victoria, obviously a favorite of hers.

RICHARD

(feeling neglected)

I'm half American, too.

VICTORIA

Merci, Madame.

8. EXT. STREET

The children coming out of the arch. They walk silently as CAMERA TRUCKS BACK before them. Victoria is absorbed in thoughts of her own; Richard is conscious of her, with a mixture of grudging admiration and jealousy.

RICHARD

Early this morning—I heard somebody on the phone.

(no answer)

Was it you?

VICTORIA
> *(evading him)*
You know we're forbidden to use the phone.

Silence a moment.

RICHARD
> I bet you don't know your lessons.

VICTORIA
> *(her thoughts far away)*
I bet I do.

Suddenly her eyes become aware of him. She can use him. Look out, Reeshard!

VICTORIA
> Except I didn't study my geography. And we have Switzerland today.

RICHARD
> *(boastful)*
Oh, Switzerland's easy. We had it.

VICTORIA
> Did you?
> *(pause)*
How far away is Hautemont, Switzerland, from Paris?

RICHARD
> *(shrugging)*
I just know the capital is Berne. The population is four million. You see, I know.

VICTORIA
> About how long does it take to get there?

RICHARD
> We didn't have to learn that.

VICTORIA
> We do.
>> *(with deceptive innocence)*
> We even have to know what railroad station we'd have to go by to get there.

RICHARD
> Well, everybody knows that—le Gare de l'Est, of course. What *we* had to know about was the chief industries—hotels, dairy products, and watches. Let's see your geography.

He reaches for Victoria's bag. She jumps aside, but he manages to heft it before she snatches it away.

RICHARD
>> *(suspicious)*
> Haven't you got your books in there?

VICTORIA
> Where would I have them?

They have reached the wall in front of her school. On the gate a copper plaque reads: ECOLE DES JEUNES FILLES

VICTORIA
> Au revoir, Reeshard.

Richard backs down the street out of the shot. Victoria steps just inside the gate, turns, and waits tensely—CAMERA REMAINING on her. Two little French girls pass her going in.

RICHARD'S VOICE
>*(over shot)*
>The area is sixteen thousand square miles. It's very mountainous.

Then Victoria snatches off her school apron, tosses it inside the gate, peers out once more, and walks back into the street.

DISSOLVE TO:

9. EXT. GARE DE L'EST (the railroad station for trains east)
10. MEDIUM SHOT—STATION ENTRANCE
—over which is carved in the stone: GARE DE L'EST. Taxis arrive in front and blue-bloused French porters carry grips slung over their shoulders. We note, particularly, A COLUMN OF LITTLE ORPHANS about Victoria's age dressed in somber brown costumes and walking two by two. At their head march two nuns who lead them into the station.

As the last of the procession disappears within, we PICK UP Victoria on the sidewalk. She is outwardly composed and serene, but the station looks very big indeed. Her glance after the last orphan is even a little envious, as if she wished that she, too, were taken care of instead of being on an adventure on her own. As she starts in—

DISSOLVE TO:

11. INT. GARE DE L'EST
General station activity. American types in evidence. We PICK UP the ORPHANS whom one nun is keeping lined up while the other one buys the tickets. Following the nun to the ticket booth we find Victoria already there. The Ticket Agent, an overbearing but not unkindly man, is glaring fiercely down at her.

AGENT
>But what part of Switzerland, Mademoiselle?

VICTORIA
>Hautemont.

20

From the Agent's face we see it is not a familiar name. The Agent looks at his price lists. Victoria glances at the Nun, who waits stiffly nearby, then back at the agent.

AGENT

> First class, three hundred francs. Second class, two hundred thirty. Third class, one hundred ninety.

Victoria fingers her purse doubtfully.

VICTORIA

> Well, I want about fifth class, I guess—or sixth.

AGENT

> Fifth class! Sixth class!
> > *(glares again)*
> You are American?

VICTORIA

> Yes, Monsieur.

AGENT

> > *(with satisfaction)*
> Ah.
> > *(draws a long breath—explodes)*
> Well, let me tell you, there is no fifth class or sixth class. Bah! The cheapest one can go to Hautemont is third class, for one hundred ninety francs!

Victoria's back is toward us. We only see the Agent from her level, enormous and ominous as he looms over her. (This is a point where the camera might be tipped up from Victoria's angle to point at the agent.)

AGENT

> > *(accusingly)*
> You see! Last week you have a stock-market crash in New York. Before that, you want to go first class de luxe, like grand dukes—like heavenly angels.

21

He makes a slight bow to the Nun, who is fairly surprised.
Then he returns to his attack on the unspeakable Victoria.

AGENT
> And now you want to go fifth class, *sixth* class! Nothing is cheap enough for you. You have to invent a *new* class!

VICTORIA
> I only have thirty francs.

He is beside himself.

AGENT
> What next?

THE NUN
> *(thinking he is addressing her)*
> Twenty-four third class to Melun, if you please, Monsieur.

AGENT
> *(to Victoria)*
> You play the market in Wall Street and now you have thirty francs left! And you come to me to let you go to Switzerland. Well, let me tell you, with fifty francs you couldn't go any farther than Melun!

The music surges up, as the CAMERA MOVES SWIFTLY BACKWARD and we see this part of the station from a WIDE ANGLE: the waiting orphans, the Little Girl turning away from the ticket window, the Nun taking her place.

DISSOLVE TO:

12. ANOTHER PART OF THE WAITING ROOM
Along the walls are bright posters of Switzerland—Lake Geneva, Lucerne, Zurich, St. Moritz, etc. In front of them stands Victoria, thoughtful but not defeated. Behind her is a door over which is a sign: DAMES. And now the proces-

sion of little Orphans goes past her headed for that door. Victoria turns from the posters and watches them idly. The sight of them gives her an idea, and she starts quickly away in another direction.

13. THE TICKET AGENT'S BOOTH

He reacts as he sees Victoria approaching.

AGENT

(*ferociously, to himself*)
Fifth class! Sixth class!

Victoria comes into shot.

VICTORIA

Is Melun on the way to Switzerland?

AGENT

(*nodding suspiciously*)
Oui.

VICTORIA

Well, would you please give me a ticket to Melun.

The Agent shrugs his shoulders and takes down a ticket.

AGENT

Twenty-five francs, ten centimes.
(*he looks at her sharply*)
But what will you do then? You think the stock market will go up again before you get there?

He puts the ticket down. Victoria places the money beside it. He taps the ticket with his finger.

AGENT

(*severely*)
When you get to Melun, where are you? What will you do?

23

Victoria picks up the ticket.

VICTORIA
Thank you.

The ticket agent stares after her.

AGENT
(*aloud, to himself*)
Well, if she rides past her stop, she must get off *some*time, and they will put her under arrest.

He folds his arms and nods Napoleonically. He has done his duty.

14. INT. STATION
Victoria putting the ticket in her purse. (The shot includes the door marked DAMES) The little Orphans, chaperoned by the Nuns, now come walking out two by two—blocking Victoria's way. On this laugh—I hope!—we

DISSOLVE TO:

15. EXT. FULL SHOT STATION QUAI (PLATFORM)
The train is ready to start. Immediately in front of us are two railroad cars. All of one car, and half of the other, contain third-class compartments, each plainly marked on the door with the Latin numeral III. The second car contains, in addition, two compartments that are marked on the door with the Latin numeral I—first class. Such an arrangement is usual in a French train.

We PICK UP Victoria coming onto the platform and advancing toward the cars of the waiting train. She takes out her ticket and looks at it.

INSERT: Victoria's ticket is plainly marked:
PARIS A MELUN—IIIme Classe [3rd class]

16. MEDIUM SHOT
Victoria starts toward the two cars in front of us. At the same moment the head of the column of Orphans, led by

the Nuns, appears between her and the cars. The action should work out as follows:

The Nuns are embarking the Orphans exactly as officers embark soldiers; that is to say, they stop the column at the door of each third-class compartment, indicate eight of their little charges and wave them in. Then move the column along to the next compartment and dispose of eight more, etc., working along the side of the cars.

We must show that Victoria's geographical position is such so that she is behind the middle of the Orphans' column and farther away from the train, so that, consequently, each of the third-class compartments are filled to the brim before she has a chance to get into any of them. In fact, there are a couple of Orphans left. These squeeze into the last of the third-class compartments, leaving absolutely no room, and leaving Victoria at a loss.

There is a law in France that if accommodation cannot be provided in the class for which a ticket has been purchased, the purchaser has a right to move up one class and take a seat therein. Victoria, of course, doesn't know this; nevertheless, common sense tells her that she has a right to get on the train, so when she sees that there is no more room in the third-class compartments, she shrugs her shoulders, opens the door of the first-class compartment adjoining, and steps in.

17. INT. FIRST-CLASS COMPARTMENT

Victoria entering—finding a rather odd group of people. Facing forward is a stout Circassian woman with a rich shawl over her head and a brood of Near-Eastern children. On her lap is an ugly boy-child of three dressed like a young Sultan sucking a big piece of candy, and on either side a boy and a girl of eleven or twelve (both slightly larger than Victoria). They are all dressed with Oriental elegance but extremely dirty, according to our ideas; their hands and faces filthy from fruits and confections.

Across from them sits a spoiled American minx of Victoria's age accompanied by a French governess. This compartment holds six people, and probably the sixth seat, which is empty, really belongs to the little child whom the Circassian lady holds in her lap. Anyhow, when Victoria comes in and sits down, there is a sudden burst of unintelligible double-talk from the four Circassians—all of them pointing to Victoria and indicating in sign language that the seat belongs to the Little Sultan who is in his mother's lap. The little American girl, whose name is Evylyn, is in a disagreeable humor.

EVYLYN
>   *(to Victoria)*
>   That's their seat.

FRENCH GOVERNESS
>   Evylyn!

EVYLYN
>   *(to Victoria)*
>   Anyhow, you're not so dirty as they are.

Victoria, surprised by the rudeness, glances at the Circassians.

EVYLYN
>   Oh, they don't understand anything.

FRENCH GOVERNESS
>   Tu vas voir. Je vais dire ça à ton Papa. [You'll see. I'm going to tell your father]

EVYLYN
>   Papa won't do anything to me. The darn fool!

FRENCH GOVERNESS
>   Evylyn!

Evylyn looks to Victoria for support, but Victoria is shocked.

EVYLYN
>   If mother always calls him a—

FRENCH GOVERNESS
>   *(desperately, to the child)*
>   S'il te plaît!

Evylyn subsides.

18. CLOSE SHOT—VICTORIA
looking out the window. Suddenly she starts, dismayed by what she sees, and shrinks back against the seat.

19. EXT. PLATFORM SHOOTING TOWARD THE TRAIN
Two men talking. The one who is *facing* the train, and whom Victoria recognizes, we cannot see—but we see the face of the one whose back is toward the train. He is a youth of nineteen, blond, weak and cruel. He wears a CLOSE-FITTING TOPCOAT.

They stroll aside a few steps, still keeping their relative positions.

20. INT FULL SHOT—COMPARTMENT
Evylyn talks to Victoria, who does not relax until she sees that the men are out of sight.

EVYLYN
>   What's your name?

VICTORIA
>   *(absently)*
>   Victoria.

EVYLYN
>   Mine's Evylyn Wilkes Bell. My father—

FRENCH GOVERNESS
                    (on guard)
          Tais-toi de ton Papa.

From this point, Victoria pays attention.

EVYLYN
                    (sulkily)
          I didn't say anything about the old—

FRENCH GOVERNESS
          Evylyn!

Victoria, thoroughly shocked, manages to speak politely.

VICTORIA
          If anything ever happened to your father, you'd feel
          differently.

Evylyn's curiosity is aroused.

EVYLYN
          Why? Did something happen to your father?

Suddenly Victoria feels that she has said too much.

EVYLYN
                    (persistently)
          Did it?

Victoria doesn't answer.

EVYLYN
                    (her curiosity increasing minute by minute)
          Did something happen to your father?

VICTORIA
          Never mind.

> (taking refuge in attack)
> All I say is, nobody should discuss their father like that.

EVYLYN

> (jumping to a guess)
> Is he dead?

VICTORIA

> No, he's not.

Her eyes fill with tears.

The Circassian family across the aisle understand nothing but feel a certain sympathy for Victoria. The little girl stands up and makes sign language that she wishes Victoria would try on her head shawl while she tries on Victoria's hat. Victoria blinks hard a moment and then agrees to the game. Evylyn turns away in disdain and looks out the window as the TRAIN STARTS MOVING.

21. EXT. PLATFORM SHOOTING TOWARD MOVING TRAIN

The YOUTH IN THE CLOSE-FITTING TOPCOAT backs away from the other and grabs a rail of the car *behind* Victoria's car and swings himself aboard. The OTHER MAN continues to stand with his back to us.

22. THE TRAIN

leaving the station.

23–27. MONTAGE SHOT

> which suggests the passing of time—about seven hours—and of space. SHOTS of a rushing train through different types of French country would do the business with the sign of the station of Melun and the Nuns and children disembarking— followed by the train going on, FLASHES OF THE SIGNS OF MORE STATIONS—one of them with a clock pointing to four.

28. INT. VICTORIA'S COMPARTMENT
Victoria is drowsing. She wakes at the sound of the train slowing down. The French Governess is looking out the window.

FRENCH GOVERNESS
>*(to Evylyn)*
The Swiss border.

29. VESTIBULE OF CAR
The train is stopping. A Swiss Customs Official swings aboard and greets the French Conductor.

SWISS OFFICIAL
>Bonjour, Monsieur. For the passport examination.

FRENCH CONDUCTOR
>Oui, Monsieur.

Swiss Official starts into the car, turns back to Conductor.

SWISS OFFICIAL
>Monsieur, there is a little runaway American girl.
>*(he waves a telegram)*
>If she's on the train, I must take her off and detain her.

At this moment, a Waiter carrying a bell, passes the French Conductor and the Swiss Official, and goes into the car ringing his bell.

WAITER
>First service for dinner!
>*(repeats ad lib)*

30. VICTORIA'S COMPARTMENT

A rich, vulgar American woman, about the type you would expect Evylyn's mother to be, puts her head in the door.

EVYLYN'S MOTHER

> I'll take Evylyn to dinner, Mademoiselle. You can eat when we get to Lausanne.

FRENCH GOVERNESS

> Oui, Madame.

Evylyn's mother looks scathingly at Victoria and pulls Evylyn past her, as if Victoria were contaminating. Victoria looks after them, hungrily. The little Circassian girl sees this. The Circassian girl produces a stock of chocolate and points to Victoria's hat. Victoria understands, accepts the chocolate, lends the little girl the hat again, and takes in return the little girl's shawl. During this, the bell-ringing Waiter goes past and looks in, but the Circassians, not understanding, pay no attention.

31. THE CORRIDOR

Swiss Official is proceeding along the aisle from compartment to compartment. He encounters Evylyn and her mother and asks to see their passports. He is very inquisitive, wondering if Evylyn could be the little girl. In the b.g. of the aisle the Conductor has also started his rounds.

32. VICTORIA'S COMPARTMENT

Victoria is deliciously tasting the chocolate bar, when the door opens and the Swiss Official puts his head in.

SWISS OFFICIAL

> Les passeports, s'il vous plaît, mesdames.

33. CLOSE-UP—VICTORIA

She is stricken. She had never thought of a passport until this minute.

34. FULL SHOT—COMPARTMENT

The mother of the Circassians takes out a huge passport, opens it, and begins jabbering in obscure double-talk to the Swiss Official. The passport contains photographs not only of the three children with her but, apparently, of about six others besides. The Swiss Official throws up his hands.

SWISS OFFICIAL
> (despairingly)
Ah-h!

He points at one of the photographs and then at one of the children.

ALL CIRCASSIANS
> (at once)
No—no—no—no—no.

Swiss Official tries again to identify photographs, then gives up. Victoria now sees her way out. She pretends to jabber, too, in a language exactly like theirs. The Swiss Official says "Ah-h!" again and leans against the door. There's absolutely nothing he can do against a lineup like this. He examines the French Governess's passport quickly, as the jabbering continues, then throws up his hands and passes out into the corridor. There he meets the Conductor. Through the glass door, we see him explaining to him the hopeless situation inside.

35. TWO SHOT—VICTORIA

The French Governess smiles at Victoria. She has guessed that Victoria has gotten over the border without a passport, but she will not tell. Victoria, encouraged by the smile, takes out her ticket.

VICTORIA
I had to get to Switzerland.

FRENCH GOVERNESS
(looking at the ticket)
But this ticket—we've passed Melun hours ago.

VICTORIA

(firmly)
I have to get to Hautemont.

The Governess has taken a great fancy to Victoria, wishes she had such a child to bring up. She says, "Oh!" suddenly because the Conductor has just opened the door. Warned by the other official, the Conductor simply stretches out his hand. One child hands him a banana, but he finally gets the tickets—except Victoria's—and withdraws hastily.

FRENCH GOVERNESS
(to Victoria)
For Hautemont, I think you change at Montreux.

36. LONG SHOT—TRAIN
—traveling through mountainous country. Important that it is *still light* outside, about six o'clock in the evening.

DISSOLVE TO:

37. THE COMPARTMENT—VICTORIA
—alone. The others have apparently disembarked; there is not even a bag left in the compartment—only orange rinds, banana skins, waxed paper—the debris of the Circassians.

Victoria, quiet but a little tense, is looking out the window. The train is rounding the long shore of Lake Geneva.

38. AISLE OF THE CAR
Along the aisle, and with no particular objective, strolls the YOUTH IN THE CLOSE-FITTING TOPCOAT. He looks idly into the vacant compartments—then into Victoria's. There is no sparkle of interest in his white, dull eyes.

39. INT. THE COMPARTMENT

Victoria's eyes are far away. And now, *without her lips moving*, we hear her own voice in the compartment.

VICTORIA'S VOICE
(softly)
It was only last Spring that we left New York—and it seems years ago.

40. THE CORRIDOR

The YOUTH IN THE CLOSE-FITTING TOPCOAT passing on slowly.

Through the glass of the compartment door in background of shot, we see Victoria.

41. THE COMPARTMENT—VICTORIA

VICTORIA'S VOICE
Daddy and Mummy and I—

FADE OUT.

SEQUENCE B

FADE IN:
42. A new scene is now DISSOLVING IN.
As Victoria's voice continues, it becomes a SHOT OF THE RICHEST SECTION OF PARK AVENUE—on a bright spring morning.

VICTORIA'S VOICE
(continuing offscene)
—started for the boat that morning.

DISSOLVE TO:

43. EXT. EXPENSIVE LIMOUSINE, MODEL 1929
—going down Park Avenue.

VICTORIA'S VOICE
We thought it'd be such fun. Mother was so happy—

DISSOLVE TO:

44. LONG SHOT—TIMES SQUARE
—moving band of lights around the Times Building reads:
—KELLOGG PEACE PACT SIGNED—100 CONVICTED ON JONES LAW—

VICTORIA'S VOICE
>—she hadn't been well, and now Daddy was taking a real vacation—retiring from the stock market for good.

45. MED. SHOT EXT. LIMOUSINE
—in a cross street.
46. FRONT SEAT OF LIMOUSINE
—showing Rowan, the chauffeur; young, well turned out.

ROWAN
(half turning about)
Was that Pier Twelve, Mr. Wales?

DISSOLVE TO:

47. EXT. STREET OUTSIDE PIER 12, NORTH RIVER
Prospective voyagers getting out of cars. The Waleses' limousine draws up and a porter runs to open the door. Victoria gets out first, carrying a small doll. CAMERA MOVES UP to Rowan getting out of the front seat. He has something on his mind.

ROWAN
(rather diffidently)
Mr. Wales—

Charles Wales comes into the shot. He is a vital, confident, immediately likable man of thirty-five. His hands are full of tickets, passports, baggage checks, etc., which he puts in the side pocket of his coat.

ROWAN
—about Du Pont de Nemours. You've been so kind
—I thought you'd tell me whether to hang on or not.

Wales's expression is first annoyed, then cynical.

36

WALES
>Done pretty well?

ROWAN
>Not bad. Thanks to you, Mr. Wales.

Wales smiles, and starts away.

ROWAN
>*(following him; rather desperately)*
>Somebody said you were getting out of the market,
>sir. And you're going abroad—

WALES
>All the more reason for my not giving tips. If the
>market rises to heaven or drops to—zero, I won't be
>here to see.
>*(looks at his watch)*
>Better get Mrs. Wales—at the hairdresser's.

He goes out of shot. CAMERA REMAINS on Rowan.

ROWAN
>*(raising his voice)*
>Well, thanks for everything, Mr. Wales.

Two Negro porters with bags hurry past Rowan.

1ST PORTER
>U.S. Steel up three.

2ND PORTER
>I got me five shares of kink-remover. Folks allus
>gonna need that.

48. EXT. THE COVERED PIER
Wales joins Victoria and they start out the pier together,

CAMERA TRUCKING in front of them. The pier is crowded with travelers and their friends. The atmosphere is joyous and excited.

VICTORIA
> Here we go, Daddy.

WALES
> We certainly do. And I'm glad of this chance to get to know you.
> *(takes off his hat)*
> I'm Charles T. Wales, Sixteen and a half Wall Street.

VICTORIA
> *(playing up)*
> I'm Victoria Wales, One ninety-five Park Avenue.

They pause in their walk and shake hands.

WALES
> Married or single?

VICTORIA
> No, not married—single.

Their Red Cap is wheeling a truckload of their baggage past them.

WALES
> *(indicating the doll in her arms.)*
> But I see you have a child, Madam.

Victoria looks at her doll, almost with surprise.

VICTORIA
> Oh, that's just a habit.

Spotting the Red Cap she puts the doll on the truck with the other baggage.

VICTORIA

>Actually, that's when I was a child. Lately, I've been reading the papers from cover to cover. I'm more interested in things like bulls and bears.

She and her father start to walk again. He smiles faintly.

VICTORIA

>Honestly, I am, Daddy. If you could just explain which is a bull and which is a bear, we could have talks like we used to.

They have come to a soft-drink stand on the pier. He indicates "Will you have one?"

VICTORIA

>Mother won't miss the boat?

Wales looks at his watch.

WALES

>No, lots of time. Meanwhile, we can pursue this acquaintance.

They order soft drinks in pantomime, are quickly served with bottles.

VICTORIA

>*(returning to her previous thought)*
>I'm behind the times for my age. I'm obsolescent.

WALES

>The word is *adolescent*—and you're *not*—yet—thank heaven!

She nods dolefully.

WALES

VICTORIA

It must be awful.

Sympathetically, Wales decides to take her at her word.

WALES

Bulls and bears, eh? Well— What does a bear do?
(*makes a gesture of clawing*)
Pulls people down. And a bull hooks them up.
(*repeats*)
Bear pulls people down, bull hooks up.

The repetition is unfortunate. The first spills his drink, the second bumps his head into a tennis-racket case that a woman is carrying past. Shaking his head at this unfortunate incident, Wales puts money on counter and they walk along.

WALES

But you're right: I've been neglecting you for months. For instance, baby, you don't carry yourself well lately.

He bends her shoulders gently backwards as they walk. CAMERA IS LOW at this point to include in a TWO SHOT all of Victoria, leaving out her father's head and shoulders. Through this shot it continues to photograph at this level.

WALES

This summer, we're going to work on your diving— that'll straighten you up.

Victoria strains her shoulders back.

WALES

> No. Push your chin straight back and then the rest of
> you falls right into place.

Victoria looks up at him and then does it correctly.

WALES

> That's better. How would you like to see anybody
> walk like this?

49. TWO SHOTS—CAMERA AT AVERAGE LEVEL
—showing Wales giving a ridiculous shambling imitation
of her walk. Victoria greets this with a delighted laughter.

VICTORIA

> Oh, *Da*ddy.

He looks about to see if anyone has noticed.

WALES

> You should try to walk like a queen.

CAMERA DESCENDS to Victoria's level.

VICTORIA

> How do queens walk?

WALES

> *(reflectively)*
> Well, I've only met one queen, and she was an awful
> stumble-bum.

Victoria smiles. They are happy.

50. ANOTHER PART OF THE PIER—CLOSE SHOT OF
    DWIGHT SCHUYLER
Schuyler's father and grandfather were in Wall Street before him. He is smooth-shaven, steady-going, firm of

countenance, and of excellent habits, as is shown by his fine physical trim. He is impeccably dressed—dark suit and tie and derby, with a white carnation as the only spot of color. He carries a silver-headed cane.

Schuyler spots Wales and starts toward him.

51. MED. SHOT—WALES AND VICTORIA WALKING
Dwight Schuyler comes into shot. In the shot also is a baby carriage that is being pushed gently to and fro by a British nurse.

SCHUYLER
> *(after a smile at Victoria)*
> 'Morning, Charles.

Victoria looks at the baby carriage curiously. While the men converse the following happens: one axle of the baby carriage sticks or catches so that the carriage will not move. It is a minor repair, and the nurse stoops to fix it. Victoria puts her hands on her knees and watches. The baby cannot be seen in shot. At the beginning, this group shot is PHOTOGRAPHED AT ADULT LEVEL.

SCHUYLER
> I suppose there's nothing more to be said.

WALES
> Nothing. I decided months ago I was going to quit. And now there's Helen, too—her nerves are going to crack if we don't get out of this town.

SCHUYLER
> *(he feels strongly about Wales's defection)*
> The moral side doesn't seem to have occurred to you —obligation to your partners—

CAMERA COMES DOWN TO VICTORIA'S LEVEL. The men's faces are out of shot.

WALES'S VOICE

(shortly)

I'm leaving you my name.

SCHUYLER'S VOICE

It's your talents we'll miss, Charles. That gift of the—
divine guess. That's why we insured your life for a
cool million.

WALES'S VOICE

(thoughtfully)

It's been fun. It's been a great time. But I want to do
other things. Helen and I want to track around Eu-
rope—

SCHUYLER'S VOICE

I realize Helen isn't well—

WALES'S VOICE

If Helen was in the pink, I'd still be getting out,
Dwight. I want a new job—exploring the poles,
climbing mountains—

52. FULL GROUP SHOT

At this point the British nurse straightens, takes up a tiny
wrapped baby, of which we only see the head, and places
it in Victoria's arm with the single low words, "Don't drop
it." Then she stoops again to the buggy. Wales's back is
turned. Schuyler doesn't notice the incident.

WALES

—five years from now, I may be punching cattle in
Mongolia—and at seventy, I may go in for Ming pot-
tery. I want to live ten lives, not just one, and I want
to begin now.

Schuyler's expression during this has been interesting. He doesn't quite understand, feeling that anybody is a fool to get out of the bull market.

SCHUYLER
(lightly)
In other words, you're quitting work.

WALES
(good-humoredly giving up)
I won't explain my point of view again. Let's say it's on account of Helen. She needs me. Let it go at that.

Victoria is taking the holding of the baby very tensely and seriously.

WALES
(continuing)
She'd probably be all right if she didn't hear the ticker in her dreams all night.

VOICE
(calling offscene)
Mr. Schuyler! Mr. Schuyler!

SCHUYLER
Yes.

Telegraph boy comes into shot and gives Schuyler a wire, which he signs for and opens as CAMERA COMES DOWN AGAIN TO VICTORIA'S LEVEL. Into the shot leaps a small dog on a leash. The dog playfully tries to jump on Victoria. She turns so that the baby is safely away.

SCHUYLER
(reading above shot)
Consolidated Nickel opens at two-o-one.

WALES
>(eagerly)
Let's see it.

Still on VICTORIA'S LEVEL we see Schuyler's hand tantalizingly hold it away.

SCHUYLER
No—you're out of it all now.

WALES
Let's see it!

He seizes it. The nurse finishes fixing the baby carriage and stands up.

WALES
>(reading; then commenting, above shot)
Gaines is forming a pool. Don't let 'em fool you.

He suddenly crumples the telegram and throws it down. Nurse takes the baby from Victoria and puts it back in the buggy, saying, "Thank you." Victoria regrets losing her charge.

WALES
>(changing to a tone of indifference)
Oh, I'm through with all that. I've guessed for you for five years.

Two well-dressed women, Mrs. Wells and Mrs. Baker, come into shot. CAMERA still at VICTORIA'S LEVEL. Show short skirts of 1929.

MRS. WELLS
Charley—and Victoria.

A woman's hand rests on Victoria's shoulder.

MRS. BAKER
>Hello, Dwight
>>*(to Victoria)*
>Hello, honey.

MRS. WELLS
>>*(to Charles Wales)*
>One more figure in the bankbook—and we'll be joining you.

WALES
>Helen ought to be here now.

CAMERA RISES to adult level.

MRS. BAKER
>She's on board. We just said good-bye to her in your stateroom.

She turns to Victoria.
53. ANOTHER ANGLE—WALES AND SCHUYLER
Victoria and the Two Women out of shot.

SCHUYLER
>I've got to get down to the Street, Charles.
>>*(almost desperately)*
>Just tell me one last thing.

WALES
>Well?

SCHUYLER
>The bull market—is it going on? Where do you stand?

WALES
>I think the market is leaderless.

>   (*pause*)
> And just so you can judge from acts instead of words,
> I want you to transfer that other two hundred thou-
> sand into Liberty Bonds.

He takes a piece of scrap paper from his pocket, writes
something on it, and hands it to Schuyler. Schuyler is
shaking his head in heartiest disapproval.

SCHUYLER
>   You want to leave three hundred and fifty thousand
>   of your money in—

WALES
>   (*nodding*)
>   That ought to answer all your questions.

Schuyler gives up and puts the memo in his pocket, as
Ames and Drew, two junior members of the firm, come
into shot. They show great respect for Wales.

DREW
>   Send us a tip now and then, Charles.

Now we hear the beating of tin gongs from the ship and in
a French accent, cries of, "All ashore that's going ashore!"
A Reporter comes into shot. Also Bill Bonniman, a small-
town banker who has come to see Wales off. Bonniman is
about forty, a good fellow. To him, Wales is bigger than
Morgan and Rockefeller rolled into one.

BONNIMAN
>   Came down from Vermont last night, Charles. Saw
>   you were sailing.

· WALES
>   (*cordially*)
>   Bill Bonniman! Wish I'd known you were in town.

REPORTER
> What do you think of copper, Mr. Wales—a last word?

Wales shakes his head.

54. ANOTHER ANGLE

Old Mr. Van Greff, reputed one of the richest men in the world, hobbles past on two canes, accompanied by valet and secretary.

REPORTER
> There goes half a billion dollars—old Van Greff.

He goes off quickly. All are impressed at the name except Wales, who is saying good-bye to Bonniman.

AMES

(to Wales)
> Boy, how we will miss you!

More gongs. Cries of "Gangplank going up!"

55. ANOTHER ANGLE—GROUP SHOT

—including the Two Women and Victoria. Wales and Schuyler shake hands. Wales and Victoria and the Two Women start off quickly. THE CAMERA REMAINS on Schuyler, whose smile fades to a frown.

56. BY THE GANGPLANK

Wales, Victoria, and the Two Women. Women embrace Wales and Victoria. More shouting of "All aboard," gongs beating, whistle blowing. Somewhere an amateur group has begun to sing "Auld Lang Syne," and the air is alive with good-byes and waving handkerchiefs. As Wales and Victoria start up the gangplank, the last people on board, we

DISSOLVE OUT AND INTO:

57–59. LONG SHOT—THE STEAMER IN MID-OCEAN

Several shots, showing the steamer by day and by night, indicating the passage of several days.

60. INT. LUXURIOUS DECK SUITE ON THE STEAMER

A drawing room; beyond, an open door leads to bedrooms and bath. The door to the outer corridor is closing with a bang, and the French steward and stewardess are staring toward it in awe. They exchange glances.

STEWARD
>Eh Bien! Did I get it that time!

He taps the side of his neck.

STEWARDESS
>You shouldn't have asked him.

During the following, the stewardess is sweeping and the steward is gathering up breakfast things.

STEWARD
>*He* didn't mind. I only asked about General Motors. But *she,* she was like a madwoman! She says I forget myself, she will report me to the purser.

Stewardess gives him a warning look.

61. ANOTHER ANGLE

Victoria coming in from the bedroom with an open envelope in her hand. She is looking for pen and ink. She crosses the room to a writing desk and sits down.

62. TWO SHOT—STEWARD AND STEWARDESS

Working close together across the room. The stewardess glances at the child and continues. The suggestion is that they are speaking in French.

STEWARDESS
>At least they are not drunk like the Americans in 3A —3B—3C.
>>*(pause)*

49

This lady is not well. I heard her say Monsieur was like a stock ticker, and she dreamed that she kept pulling the little strip of paper out of his mouth. Pulling and pulling and pulling, and no end.

63. THE DESK
Victoria looks up from the envelope that she is addressing.
64. FULL SHOT—THE ROOM

STEWARDESS
And he laughed and she stood there, and she kept pulling and pulling—

She grabs the steward's hair and he gives a yelp, whereupon Victoria laughs and they turn toward her.

STEWARDESS
(disturbed)
You understand French, Mademoiselle?

VICTORIA
A little.

STEWARDESS
(cautiously)
You won't repeat this, a petite demoiselle like you?

Victoria shakes her head reassuringly. The telephone rings. Victoria answers.

VICTORIA
(on phone)
I'll be right up, Daddy.

She picks up her camera and starts out.
65. EXT. SPORTS DECK OF THE STEAMER
Charles Wales (not in sports costume) leans against the rail

watching a game of deck tennis. A rope ring comes sailing out of the field of play; he catches it with a quick, nervous motion before it goes over the rail and tosses it back into the ring.

A PLAYER
>Thank *you*!

Victoria comes into shot.

VICTORIA
>*(casually)*
>Where's Mother?

WALES
>She's playing bridge.

Near them a passenger is throwing bread to a flock of gulls that follows the ship. The gulls swoop down for it.

WALES
>*(to Victoria)*
>They follow all the way across for the refuse.

They watch.

WALES
>Shall we get something to feed them?

As they start away,

DISSOLVE TO:

66. ANTEROOM OF THE DINING SALON
Elevators and stairs lead down to it on either side. In front of the dining-room entrance is a great display table of food on which are laid out glistening hors d'oeuvres, salads in aspic, game, timbales, mousselines, and croustades of prawn, crab, and lobster. There are out-of-season vegeta-

bles, caviar on ice, pasties, pies, fois gras in loaves, etc., etc., all beautifully garnished so that the gourmet may quicken his appetite in anticipation. It is half an hour before lunchtime. The Maître d'Hôtel waits outside, and waiters pass to and fro.

Charles Wales and Victoria come into shot. The Maître d'Hôtel greets them with respectful politeness. Will they come in?

WALES
> We'd like lunch for some gulls. Can you get us some crackers or bread or—

MAITRE D'HOTEL
> But certainly, Monsieur Wales.
> *(to a waiter)*
> Vite! Apportez ce monsieur du pain. [Bring this gentleman some bread.]

Waiter goes off. Victoria is fascinated by the display table, particularly by a sailing ship that the chef has carved out of icing.

Old Mr. Van Greff hobbles into shot on two canes. He is bound for early lunch. Behind him is his valet. Victoria is in his path.

VICTORIA
> *(stepping aside)*
> Excuse me.

Maître d'Hôtel is again galvanized into servile activity even topping his deference to Wales. Van Greff sees Wales. After a moment he places him and stops his march.

VAN GREFF
> Charles Wales?

WALES
> *(politely)*
> Hello, Mr. Van Greff.

VAN GREFF
> Lunch?

WALES
> *(shaking his head)*
> Thank you, sir.

VAN GREFF
> You're afraid I'll nag at you to come in with me.
> Afraid you'll weaken.

Wales smiles and changes the subject.

WALES
> How have you been, sir?

VAN GREFF
> Well, every year I go to Switzerland—to die. And it
> never happens. It's very monotonous.
> *(he starts to hobble into dining room, then turns)*
> It's up on a mountain, convenient for the angels.

Maître d'Hôtel and valet follow him. When Van Greff is
out of hearing, Victoria whispers to her father.

VICTORIA
> Supposing he had to go down.
> *(she points down)*

WALES
> *(smiling)*
> Oh, that's a cinch.

The Captain of the steamer, a handsome Frenchman of fifty, comes into shot.

CAPTAIN
Bonjour, Monsieur Wales—et Mademoiselle.

He shakes hands gravely with Victoria.

At this point the CAMERA COMES DOWN AND REMAINS at Victoria's level during the ensuing dialogue. She has finished her inspection of the pastry ship and resisted an inclination to eat a piece of it. She touches the little French flag at the stern, after which she puts her hands behind her back to keep them out of harm's way.

CAPTAIN
(to Wales)
Perhaps some day I can show you the ship, Monsieur Wales. I was telling Mr. Van Greff that you financiers don't know our world—and we don't know yours. For instance, the other day I heard that shipping stocks are going up. Now I wonder what a man like you thinks?

During this, Victoria has discovered a pig's head with an apple in its mouth. She pulls her eyes down close to it and moved her teeth as if she were biting the apple.

CAMERA RISES to adult level as the waiter comes into scene and offers Wales a loaf of French bread on a plate. Wales thanks him wordlessly.

The Captain would like to continue the conversation.

CAPTAIN
Do you know, we have a fully equipped Brokers' Office on board?

CAMERA BACK to Victoria's level, as her father takes her hand.

CAPTAIN (cont.)
>Phone service from New York, London and Paris.

WALES
>I'm on vacation, Captain.

The Captain laughs politely as if he didn't quite believe this. Victoria bows to the pig as she is gently pulled away.

DISSOLVE TO:

67. HALL OF THE SHIP
Wales and Victoria walk along with a loaf of bread. A sound of drunken wassail in one of the cabins, and a fat, blondined woman accompanied by a gigolo, both stewed, stagger halfway out into the corridor. Wales and Victoria have trouble in passing.

FAT WOMAN
>*(glumly)*
>Hello, little girl.

GIGOLO
>S'nursery.

Annoyed, Wales gently urges the gigolo aside with the flat of his hand; because of the man's juxtaposition with the fat woman this pushes her into the cabin too. Wales quickly shuts the door on them.

Covering the brief episode, Wales straightens Victoria's shoulders again. They pass the broad double door of the Brokerage Office with the firm's name on frosted glass. Victoria looks curiously inside as they walk on.

68. EXT. DOOR OPENING ON DECK
CAMERA PICKS UP Wales and Victoria coming out on deck.

They stand near the rail. While he looks for gulls, she focuses her camera and snaps his picture *casually.*

VICTORIA
Was there a stock ticker in there that makes that "clack-clack-clack" all the time?

WALES
What? Oh yes. Yes, there was. I'll bet you've forgotten the difference between bulls and bears.

VICTORIA
(doubtfully; getting it wrong as she tries to illustrate it)
No, I haven't. The bear reaches *up* and the bull sticks his head *down.*
(she gives up)
Do you really *have* to know that?

She wants passionately to please him—to be a companion to him.

VICTORIA (cont.)
What else are you interested in?

WALES
Well—how about foreign places?

VICTORIA
Will we go up on that old man's mountain? I could take some fine pictures of us up there.

WALES
We'll take fine pictures everywhere—
(a tone of mock regret)
except on the Cannibal Islands.

VICTORIA
Why not there?

WALES

> *(appealing to her reason)*
> How can you take pictures while I'm eating you?—
> like I've always wanted to do.

VICTORIA

> I've gotten too old for that brand of joke, Daddy.

VICTORIA (cont.)

> *(still trying to be interesting to him)*
> Daddy, could I see a stock ticker just once, with the
> paper coming out of it?

WALES

> *(holding up the bread)*
> The gulls.

VICTORIA

> We could do that afterwards.

DISSOLVE TO:

69. BROKERAGE OFFICE ON SHIP

Typical 1929 activity. The market has presumably just
opened in New York, and thirty or forty passengers, among
them several women, are in the room. It is due to be a big
day, and the boys are already working hard posting up the
changes in the stocks on a blackboard that fills an entire
wall. There is little indication that we are on shipboard
except that the stock boys are French and wear ship's uni-
forms. Men are writing telegrams, and white-coated pages
stand by to carry them to the cable office.

Charles Wales and Victoria go to a ticker in the corner.

WALES

> Here's the little fellow that talks so big.

CAMERA now COMES DOWN to Victoria's level and STAYS there throughout the following scene. The ticker clacks three or four times emitting some tape. Victoria picks up the tape and in a CLOSE SHOT, including her hand and head, we see her read it. HOLD this an instant. Wales's hand comes into shot above hers, picking up the tickertape.

WALES'S VOICE
(over shot)
It's written in ancient Greek, you see, because we stockbrokers speak all languages.

VICTORIA
It's not my idea of Greek.

Silence a moment. We see Wales's hand take up a few more inches of the tape.

WALES'S VOICE
(somewhat abstractedly)
What? Sure, it's Greek. It says here how Pandora opened the box. Remember about Pandora?

VICTORIA
Oh, yes. She opened the forbidden box and all the misfortunes and Furies flew out.

Wales's hand take up more tape. The machine clacks again convulsively. Again silence.

WALES'S VOICE
(low but explosive)
Good Lord! They're pounding Radio! Poor old Bill Bonniman!

VICTORIA
I like about Pandora, don't you? But, of course, she shouldn't have opened the box.

WALES'S VOICE
> *(now far away)*
> What? Oh, of course not.
> *(calls off in a louder tone)*
> Page, will you get me a telegraph form?

The ticker clacks a couple of times. Wales's hand takes up the tape eagerly. He looks off.

70. A CLOCK ON THE WALL

standing at one o'clock. EFFECT: Clock hands moving forward two hours. CAMERA PANS DOWN from clock to table beside ticker. On it still rests the loaf of bread that was to have fed the gulls.

CAMERA PANS TO MEDIUM SHOT: THE BROKERAGE OFFICE.

Charles Wales is established in one of the rear chairs. At one side of him is a Stock Boy, at the other a Page.

STOCK BOY
> *(to Wales)*
> A telephone in here, Monsieur?

PAGE
> *(to Wales)*
> Monsieur Wales, this message is from a lady in the card room.

WALES
> *(taking it absently, his eyes on the stock board)*
> All right. All right.

He slips the message into the side pocket of his coat and raises his eyes to the stock board.

DISSOLVE TO:

71–74. A MONTAGE
> (a) Ship-to-shore telephone service making connections with New York Brokerage Office. (b) Ship's Brokerage Office midnight. Trading fever-

ish. (c) Ship's Brokerage Office in morning being aired and swept out. (d) Ship's "newspaper" being mimeographed or printed with date, July 3, and stock market heading: ANOTHER SIX-MILLION-SHARE DAY IN WALL STREET.

75. SECTION OF THE BROKERAGE OFFICE—NEXT DAY
A group has begun to gather around Wales watching his eyes, his every move. Again a Page delivers a message to him; he glances at it.

WALES
(utterly absorbed)
Tell Mrs. Wales I can't come now.

76. INT. SHIP'S DOCTOR'S OFFICE
In the outer room are Victoria and a French-trained nurse. Through an open door to the inner office we see the Ship's Doctor.

NURSE
(to Victoria)
The doctor will take the medicine to your mother. Is your father with her?

VICTORIA
No, he's busy.
(pause)
I think we just make her more nervous.

Victoria goes out. The Doctor comes out from the inner office and nods significantly.

DOCTOR
One—two—three of those cases on every trip.
(he makes a slow motion of delicately
tearing something)
Nerves like tissue paper. Has Mrs. Wales been ill long?

60

NURSE
> *(arranging his medicine case)*
> The little girl was noncommittal. I do not think she's
> very close to her mother.

The Doctor is leaving the room. He speaks lightly but with
implication.

DOCTOR
> I am glad now that I didn't marry that rich American
> in 1925.

77. A CORRIDOR OF THE SHIP—VICTORIA
reaching the door of the Waleses' suite, cautiously opening it, and putting her head inside.

VICTORIA
> The Doctor's coming, Mother.

As if someone beckoned her inside, she goes in.
78. INT. CABIN—SHOOTING TOWARD THE DOOR
—showing Victoria with her back against the door.

VICTORIA
> I hope you feel better.
> *(pause; she gets no answer.*
> *We hear a match struck)*
> I'll be up in the playroom, so don't worry. Good-bye.

She starts out.
79. THE CORRIDOR—FOLLOW VICTORIA ALONG
She passes the brokers' office, pauses, looks inside. She is
not upset. Her father has always played the market, her
mother has for a long time been rather odd. But she sighs;
she is not seeing anything of her father, after all. She
passes along the corridor.

61

79.A THE CAMERA LEAVES HER,
turns on its own axis, and looks into the brokerage office. Wales is sitting there in a busy crowd, a highball beside his hand. He is not at all drunk but he is both stimulated and tired. A group is gathered around him composed of parasites, acquaintances and the merely curious. Wales is a hero to them.

GROUP AD LIBS
> You sure rigged it, old boy. You play the market by ear, Mr. Wales, but you sure can play! Man, they're running for cover.

Wales turns to a Page at his elbow.

WALES
> Go and see where Mrs. Wales is.

PAGE
> Yes, sir.

80. CORNER OF THE CARD ROOM
Three women at a bridge table with an unopened deck and a deck being shuffled.

1st WOMAN
> We've waited an hour. Let's find another fourth.

THE CAMERA ANGLE WIDENS to show Victoria passing near the card table.

2nd WOMAN
> Victoria, do you know if your mother is going to play with us this afternoon?

VICTORIA
> (politely)
> She's not feeling very well.

81. BROKERAGE OFFICE

Activity at its highest pitch. Wales with the light of battle in his eye. The market is closing any minute. An admiring group around Wales. (This mustn't be overdone.)

AN ONLOOKER
> *(almost savagely)*
> Finish 'em off.

Wales looks at him rather distantly. He stands up.

WALES
> No . . . I was just trying to help a friend of mine. I think he's all right now. I'm through.

A Page comes into shot, stands at his elbow.

PAGE
> I can't find Mrs. Wales.

A deck steward comes into shot on the other side.

DECK STEWARD
> Mrs. Wales isn't on deck or in the card room. She was in the bar an hour ago. She hasn't been in her suite.

82. CABIN OF A SHIP'S OFFICER

The Doctor stands by the Ship's Officer, bag in hand, with a worried expression. A Deck Steward in shot.

SHIP'S OFFICER
> *(to Deck Steward)*
> Cherchez par tout le bateau. Il faut trouvez Madame Wales.
> [Look all over the boat. We *must* find Mrs. Wales.]

DECK STEWARD
    Oui, mon lieutenant.

83. CHILDREN'S PLAYROOM

Small children are on a seesaw. Older children are playing ball. Victoria stands nearby but has not joined in—she doesn't feel gay.

84. MONTAGE EFFECT: CHARLES WALES'S FACE
Very distraught, with other faces around him—all speaking to him.

VOICES
    Not here, Mr. Wales.
    Not there, Mr. Wales.
    Not in her room.
    Not in the bar, Mr. Wales.
    Not in there, Mr. Wales.

Throughout this, the ship's dance orchestra is playing tunes of 1929 in a nervous rhythm.

85. A DARK SKY FILLED WITH SEA GULLS

The sudden sound of a wild shriek—which breaks down after a moment, into the cry of the gulls as they swoop in a great flock down toward the water. Through their cries we hear the ship's bell signaling for the engines to stop.

86. MEDIUM SHOT—STERN OF THE SHIP
Ship receding from the camera as the awful sounds gradually die out.

                FADE OUT.

FADE IN:

87. LONG SHOT—THE FRENCH PORT OF LE HAVRE
—with the steamship entering the harbor—with the superimposed title:

LE HAVRE, FRANCE—JULY 4

During this shot and at intervals during the following scenes, we hear the sounds of Sousa marches: "The Stars and Stripes Forever," "The High School Cadet," etc., played by the ship's band.

88. LONG SHOT—THE SHIP DOCKING

—shooting from the angle of those waiting on the pier. Band music loud and spirited.

89. BEHIND THE PICKET BARRIER

Pierre and Marion Petrie waiting in the crowd. He is a Frenchman with a military tradition that makes him pompous and ceremonious in his personality—but when he had taken off his uniform, back in 1919, it was apparent that nature had equipped him to be only a minor clerk.

His wife Marion (Helen Wales's sister) is an extremely pretty American woman of thirty-two who must have hoped for a better match. She is now in a state of great emotion—barely controlled. She is agitated almost to the breaking point by the news of her sister's suicide, which reached her last night in Paris. Always before this she has felt a certain secret jealousy of her sister, who has had great wealth and luxury. Now suddenly this has changed into a wild hatred of Charles Wales, whom she makes the scapegoat of the catastrophe. In a few hours she has fully convinced herself that her sister was the dearest thing in life to her.

Petrie's grief is mingled with awe. There has always been something so magnificent about his brother-in-law, Charles Wales, that even Helen Wales's suicide seems on a magnificent scale.

Marion is dressed in black hasty mourning. Pierre wears a much-worn morning coat, a derby, and carries a wrapped umbrella like a sword. Their eyes are fixed with fascination upon the approaching boat.

Local newsboys are passing along with the Paris papers, including *New York Herald, Fourth of July Edition,* under their arms. One of them approaches Pierre and Marion Petrie. Sensing that Marion is American, he digs out a *New York Herald* and holds it toward her. The headline reads:

Marion shrinks back. Pierre puts his arm around her.

PETRIE
>   Courage, courage.

NEWSBOY
>   *(pointing off)*
>   S'est jetée de ce bateau! [Threw herself from this ship!]

PETRIE
>   *(with a fierce gesture)*
>   Allez-vous en! [Get on with you!]

The people next to the Petries buy papers eagerly. Very faintly, we hear:

MARION
>   Oh, poor Helen! Oh, sister, sister!

PETRIE
>   Courage! Remember the little girl.

MARION
>   I can't bear to see him! He drove her to it.

PETRIE
>   No, no, you mustn't say such things.

90. BESIDE THE SHIP
The gangplank is going down. A crowd is already on the debarkation deck waiting to come on shore.

91. FULL SHOT OF THOSE WAITING ON THE DOCK
Not very many, perhaps fifty. Nothing like the reception or departure crowds in New York. CAMERA PICKS UP some re-

porters alighting from an automobile and joining the line
—there are two or three men, one woman, and several
photographers.

92. CLOSE SHOT—A PHOTOGRAPHER DOUBTFULLY FITTING IN A BULB

PHOTOGRAPHER

Tell this guy these gadgets are new—they're being
tried out on him.

SOB SISTER

Get me a good one of the little girl, will you, Jack? A
close-up?

93. THE GANGPLANK

First passengers coming down. From an aperture in the
ship's hold trunks are already being wheeled out and deposited on the dock.

94. THE PETRIES

MARION

(her face working)
I can't stand this. We should have waited in Paris.

PETRIE

(terribly agitated himself)
I think I see them.

He peers.

95. BESIDE THE SHIP

People disembark endlessly but not yet a sign of Victoria
or her father. In this shot we distinguish the Newsboy.

NEWSBOY

(crying out)
Stocks de Wall Street. Les Hotels de Paris! [Wall
Street stocks. Paris Hotels.]

96. CLOSER SHOT OF THE GANGPLANK

French Ship's Officer standing beside it. The American newspaper delegation is separating out a few celebrities from the crowd and photographing them. One of the newsmen approaches the Ship's Officer.

> NEWSPAPERMAN
>
> Now about Charles Wales and his daughter? They coming off this way?

> SHIP'S OFFICER
> *(rather impatiently)*
> That's not your affair.

> NEWSPAPERMAN
> *(arrogantly)*
> Your line likes publicity, doesn't it?

Disgustedly, Ship's Officer looks away.

97. FULL SHOT—THE DOCK

The crowd on gangplank has now thinned, the passengers are scattered around the dock as the examination of baggage begins.

98. HEAD OF THE GANGPLANK

—shooting along the debarkation deck. CAMERA GOES SWIFTLY ALONG THE DECK. Far down we see a group approaching. At the head is Charles Wales.

Twenty-four hours have made him into a different man. He is like one in a dream. There is a stubble of beard on his face, his eyes are bloodshot as if he hadn't slept, and his mouth is slightly ajar in a sort of suspended horror. He walks with a slack, listless step—like a man who has passed through hell and is going to his execution. A little behind him on one side walks the Captain of the ship, and on the other side, the Ship's Doctor, both with a solemn tread. Behind them walks Victoria, her child's face very serious. She carries her camera and her small suitcase. She is accompanied on one side by the Ship's Nurse, on the other by the Stewardess whom we have seen before. The Room Steward brings up the rear of the procession.

It reaches the head of the gangplank. Victoria's eyes at this point are fixed on her father. He is what she has left now, and in a dim way she already realizes it. The party starts down the gangplank.

99. SECTION OF THE WAITING CROWD—FAVORING THE PETRIES
—who have left their place and are trying to get through the barrier, which is now open.

100. MED. SHOT—CENTERING ON CHARLES WALES
—and showing the mournful cortege descending the gangplank. At the foot of the gangplank, as the Captain shakes hands with him, the first newspaperman comes up.

1st NEWSPAPERMAN
Mr. Wales, with the greatest sympathy, I want to ask you for a statement. Could you tell us if your wife had been ill—

He breaks off as Wales slowly turns to him, his expression changing from one of inner absorption to shock, and then to terrible resentment.

WALES
No! Please let me alone.

Meanwhile, the photographers have snapped Victoria, who covers her eyes with both knuckles after the flash of the bulb. Wales goes up to the photographer and hits him a fumbling inept blow on the chest—simply a half delirious "get-out-of-my-way," *not* a sock. He has put his hand momentarily around Victoria's shoulder, but he walks on alone with Victoria a few feet behind. The newspaperman trails him. The Doctor touches the newspaperman on his elbow.

DOCTOR

S'il vous plaît, Monsieur.

1st NEWSPAPERMAN

All right, all right.

VICTORIA

(calling after her father)

Daddy!

Wales stops. He turns around. He looks at Victoria, as if she wasn't there. Into the shot comes a French chauffeur.

CHAUFFEUR

Monsieur Wales, I have the car to drive you to Paris. If you have your trunk keys—?

101. A LITTLE WAY OFF

Marion is kneeling with Victoria in her arms. Victoria is holding the camera out over Marion's shoulder rather awkwardly. Victoria's face is grave, serious. Petrie stands over them shaking his head from side to side.

102. WALES AND THE CHAUFFEUR

CHAUFFEUR

—I'll have your luggage through the Customs in no time.

Chauffeur goes out of shot. Other passengers look up from their trunks at Wales. The group of newspaper people are gathered together, looking at him. His face is twisted with nerves and, realizing this, he sets it firmly and simply stands there in a new mood of something like defiance. What's going on inside him is the feeling, "Could I have prevented this awful thing? Could I have stopped it? Yes, I *might* have stopped it. Therefore, am I to blame? Would she be here alive except for me?" And side by side with this he has the awful pounding realization that wherever the blame lies, he has lost Helen forever.

103. GROUP SHOT—THE PETRIES AND VICTORIA

Victoria sees her father over Marion's shoulder. Her face during most of this has been sad but expressionless, but the sight of her father standing there, so alone, frightens her and at the same time seems to call to her.

VICTORIA
(to Marion)
There's Daddy.

MARION
(weeping)
Oh, my baby.

Petrie draws himself up and, with resolution, tinged with trepidation, starts off toward Wales. Victoria starts slowly and uncertainly after him. Marion makes a move to restrain her; then her hand falls to her side. The CAMERA MOVES AHEAD with Petrie, PANNING him into a shot with Wales.

Wales for an instant hardly seems to recognize Petrie, who grasps his hand quietly.

PETRIE
Ah, Charles—ah, Charles.

WALES
(automatically)
Hello, Pierre.

He looks around, sees Marion for the first time. His immediate instinct is to share his grief with her. His face almost lightens for a moment as he starts toward her.

104. GROUP SHOT—WALES FOLLOWED BY PETRIE COM-
ING INTO SHOT WITH MARION—VICTORIA NOT
IN SHOT

WALES
                    (almost with appeal)
       Marion.

Marion stands up. She is the impersonation of outrage and
hatred, which she hides under a thin mantle of pity and an
air of accepting something inevitable that she had always
foreseen.

MARION
                    (her lips scarcely moving)
       Hello, Charles.

Wales stares at her—getting it.

WALES
       Will you take Victoria for a while?

Marion nods.

WALES
       I have a car here.

MARION
                    (quickly)
       Oh, we have our return tickets to Paris. Victoria can
       go with us.

PETRIE
       Perhaps it would be better—

Wales looks at him, and Petrie breaks off.

72

WALES
>*(to Marion, quickly and with an effort)*
>They stopped the ship. They searched for hours.

MARION
>*(in a loud, almost hysterical voice)*
>Please! Please!

The band breaks out now into a Sousa march, something triumphant and patriotic. In a group near them, someone is shooting off Roman candles into the afternoon air. A man in the uniform of an American Legionnaire passes by, pinning American flags on people, and he pins one on Wales, who looks at him without understanding. The man takes the flag away and puts it on Petrie.

PETRIE
>Qu'est-ce que c'est? Je suis Français. [What's this? I'm French.]

105. ANOTHER ANGLE—CHARLES WALES'S CHAUFFEUR
—standing at the front of the tonneau of a Rolls-Royce. He takes off his cap.

106. GROUP SHOT
Marion and Charles Wales approaching, Petrie a few feet behind.

107. GROUP SHOT—TOWARD THE CAR
—showing that Victoria is sitting in the backseat. As the others come into shot, the chauffeur opens the door for Wales, spreading the light dust robe over Victoria's knees and leaving part of it open for Wales.

MARION
>*(to Victoria)*
>You're coming to Paris with us by train, dear.

Victoria has already guessed something like this without daring to admit it to herself. She looks with scarcely concealed dismay between her aunt and her father.

VICTORIA
        Daddy—

WALES
                        (with difficulty)

        It's better for you to go to Paris with your aunt.
108. VERY CLOSE SHOT—VICTORIA
She is trying hard to stifle her sobs and bending over in order to do so. She wipes her eyes very quickly and deftly on a piece of the robe before straightening up. WIDENING THE SHOT a little we see the friendly chauffeur lending her a little of the robe for this purpose, such as one might lend a handkerchief. Then Victoria gets out quickly, accidentally kicking her little camera onto the dock. She does not notice it.

WALES
        Good-bye, dear.

VICTORIA
        Daddy, Daddy, will I—

PETRIE
                        (puts his hand on Victoria's shoulder)
        You'll see your father.

VICTORIA
        But, Daddy, when will I—

She begins to cry, great convulsive sobs without sound. It is not only the loss of her father at this particular moment that has broken her but the accumulated stress of the twenty-four hours. The band is very loud now. An electric truck heavily loaded with trunks is passing.

109. CLOSE SHOT—THE CAMERA

—crushed under the weight of the truck. No one sees.

110. CHARLES WALES—IN THE CAR

He sinks back, his eyes staring again.

CHAUFFEUR
> Hotel Ritz, Monsieur?

WALES
> What? Yes.

111. MEDIUM SHOT—THE DOCK

The Petries starting away with Victoria between them. This discloses old Mr. Van Greff with his two canes. He is about to get into a waiting limousine, aided by his valet. He is shaking his head from side to side and saying in a cracked voice:

VAN GREFF
> Terrible—
>> *(shakes his head again)*
> terrible!

FADE OUT.

SEQUENCE C

112. MONTAGE

Composed of copies of the *New York Herald* (Paris Edition)—featuring headlines such as:

FOUR HUNDRED AMERICANS ARRIVE ON AQUITANIA
THREE HUNDRED FIFTY AMERICANS ARRIVE ON ILE DE FRANCE
TWO HUNDRED AMERICANS ARRIVE ON STATENDAM
SIX HUNDRED AMERICANS ON MAJESTIC

The dates of the newspapers run from July 5, 1929 to July 20, 1929. We must show that several weeks have passed.

DISSOLVE TO:

113. EXT. THE SAME PARIS APARTMENT HOUSE THAT WE SHOWED IN SEQUENCE A

DISSOLVE TO:

114. INT. HALL OF THE PETRIES' APARTMENT
Early afternoon. The hall is empty. Over the shot we hear:

MARION'S VOICE
You can't expect Victoria to learn perfect French in two weeks.

RICHARD'S VOICE
But she should try, shouldn't she, Maman?

CAMERA AFTER ESTABLISHING HALL moves into living room. All the things in it are very well worn, inherited from Pierre Petrie's parents—stiff Louis Quinze chairs, a heavy *secretaire*, a case of French books—while Marion's taste is indicated by a few modern pictures. All in all a comfortable apartment—*without any lavishness.*

In the living room are the two children and Marion, who has been marketing and carries a string reticule. Marion is in half mourning.

VICTORIA
                    (*politely*)
But, Aunt Marion, there are things I *think* in English that I don't know the words for in French.

RICHARD
                    (*scornfully*)
What things? All about how rich everything is in America? The French don't adore money like the Americans, do they Maman?

MARION
                    (*without smiling*)
No. Of course we haven't got so much to adore.

RICHARD
But we wouldn't adore it if we did have it, would we, Maman?

Marion is not so sure about this. This meal, for instance, she will cook herself because she can afford only a peasant in the kitchen. She hands the reticule to Richard to take into the kitchen—and he goes out of shot. Marion looks at Victoria sadly but lovingly. To her Victoria is the image of her martyred sister. She gently touches her hair.

VICTORIA
> *(taking advantage of Richard's absence)*
> Aunt Marion, is Father better?

The question annoys Marion. She is a decent woman and not yet prepared to admit that she would like to separate father and daughter, but that's exactly what she would like.

MARION
> *(shortly)*
> I don't think so.

VICTORIA
> What's the matter? Is he just so sorry?

MARION
> *(incredulous)*
> Sorry!

She looks at Victoria, then, realizing that she shouldn't have said this, dodges around the question.

MARION
> *(continuing)*
> Your father's had a breakdown. You see—making money, making money—then a breakdown!

Victoria is silent, considering this.

MARION
> *(continuing almost impatiently)*
> You mustn't think too much about it. Your uncle calls every few days at the Ritz Hotel.

> *(the word Ritz offends her
> and she repeats it almost savagely).*
> Ritz Hotel!

VICTORIA

> At least he might telephone.

MARION

> I believe you think more about your father than
> about your—poor mother.

Victoria tries to think this out. She is looking out the window.

VICTORIA

> *(speaking slowly)*
> Mother's dead—Daddy's still alive.

Sound of a hall door opening.
115. FRONT HALL
Petrie coming in excitedly. He has on his business clothes
now, striped trousers and a short black coat and the same
black derby. He is filled with excitement and impatient to
tell Marion the news. CAMERA FOLLOWS HIM into the living
room.

PETRIE

> *(to Marion)*
> Bonjour, ma chère.
> *(to Victoria)*
> Ma petite.
> *(to Marion).*
> Mr. Dwight Schuyler, Charles's partner, has arrived
> in Paris. He was in the office not two hours ago.

Victoria is interested.

MARION
(rather shrewishly)
Well! Perhaps he can—straighten him out.

Petrie warns her with his eyes that Victoria is within hearing.

PETRIE
He went to see Charles right away and he's coming here—to see—
(to Victoria)
Ma petite, you know Mr. Dwight Schuyler.

VICTORIA
(indifferently)
Yes.

PETRIE
(who has developed a genuine affection for Victoria)
He's coming to see you. Ah, they are rich, these Americans, rich, rich!

He passes his hand along the books.

PETRIE
(continuing)
Ah, the poor French. We have the intelligence—but money—

He sinks down gloomily into an armchair.

PETRIE
He gave the doorman twenty francs.
(pained, he repeats)
Twenty francs! Poor France.

A buzzer from downstairs peals from the pantry. Marion, conscious of how she looks, rushes for her bedroom. CAM-

ERA MOVES to the door to pantry which Richard has just opened to come into the living room. We see a raw Breton servant girl talking into one of the old-fashioned house phones.

SERVANT
    Monsieur Dwy—sky?

She puts her head into the living room, moves her mouth slowly, rehearsing her line, and then announces to Petrie.

SERVANT
    Monsieur Dwy—sky en bas.

PETRIE
    Qu'il monte tout de suite! [He is to come up right away!]

Servant returns to phone.
116. CLOSE SHOT—VICTORIA

VICTORIA
               (hopefully)
    He's been to see Daddy.

117. ANOTHER ANGLE—INCLUDING PETRIE, VICTORIA, AND RICHARD

PETRIE
      (kindly, a little embarrassed)
    Try not to mention your Papa too much in front of your aunt.

VICTORIA
    Why not?

RICHARD
> *(heedlessly)*
> Because he's drunk, you realize.

PETRIE
> *(angrily)*
> Tais toi! For shame!

Victoria looks stricken. Richard is squelched—looks from one to the other uncomfortably. Petrie turns and goes toward hall—CAMERA PANNING WITH HIM a little to leave children out of shot.

118. MARION COMING OUT OF BEDROOM
Shot includes the two children. Marion smiles at Victoria, pulls her dress into shape. Victoria is still shocked by what Richard has said.

119. TWO SHOT
Petrie and Schuyler entering living room. CAMERA PANS WITH THEM to the others.

SCHUYLER
> Mrs. Petrie. I don't think I've had the pleasure.
> *(heartily)*
> Hello there, Victoria.

Shakes hands with Richard. Schuyler is in a different mood from when we last met him on the dock in New York. Then he was hurt at Charles Wales's desertion. Now his eyes are as bright as his silver-headed cane. In the bull market stocks have continued to rise and money has been easy to make without Wales's help.

VICTORIA
> Have you seen Daddy?

SCHUYLER
> I did and I'm going to see him again.

VICTORIA
                    (eagerly)
        Can I go with you?

SCHUYLER
        Why, I think so.

                    MARION
TOGETHER   I don't know if—
                    VICTORIA
                    Oh, that's wonderful!

SCHUYLER
        Yes, I had quite a session with Charles.
        (he speaks now almost as a superior, one who is talking
        about a broken man. In fact what his voice suggests is
                    "poor old Charles")
        He seems to be *fairly* well taken care of—but I see
        room for improvement. In fact I've taken a few steps.

In sign language he indicates to Marion and Pierre that he
could talk more freely if the children weren't in the room,
whereupon Marion says to them:

MARION
        You should be over in the Luxembourg Gardens.

VICTORIA
        But if Mr. Schuyler is going to take me to see
        Daddy—

RICHARD
        Let's go in my room and play stock exchange.

As the children leave the room, Marion motions Schuyler
to sit down.

SCHUYLER

Well, the truth is that old Charles is in pretty bad
shape. He seems to have been sucking a bottle ever
since the—

(he stops delicately)

—In fact, he's gone to pieces.

MARION

(tensely)

Then why take Victoria—?

SCHUYLER

(interrupting)

Oh, I don't mean he's violent. He seems to have lost
his grip. He babbles about all the things that he and
Helen were going to do—you see, it's the first bad
break he's ever had in his life, and he's taking it—
taking it hard, would be putting it mildly. He won't
let you mention business—I'm to take care of everything.

He looks at them closely, trying to get their reaction to
what he's saying. It hasn't taken Schuyler long to realize
that Marion is the more intelligent of the two and, also that
Marion hates Charles Wales with deadly hatred.

MARION

Can't you put him in a sanitarium—straighten him
out?

SCHUYLER

(reluctantly)

Well, we'd hardly like to do that.

(pause)

I think we'd just better let things run their course.

MARION

He won't ask for Victoria?

SCHUYLER

Oh, I think not—I'm sure not.
> *(pause)*

We could probably arrange a guardianship.

MARION

> *(the legal word means little to her)*

Helen would have wanted me to bring up Victoria—
I know that.

Schuyler stands up.

SCHUYLER

Now, I'm sailing back tomorrow on the *Ile de France*.

PETRIE

> *(admiringly)*

You Americans certainly do things quick.

SCHUYLER

And I'm going to keep a special watch on all his
affairs. You take care of the little girl.
> *(calling off)*

Victoria!

120. ANOTHER ANGLE—GROUP SHOT

—with Victoria running out of the bedroom. She has her
hat and very light coat on.

SCHUYLER

> *(continuing)*

I'll bring her back safely. I thought you two might
like to dine with me in some quiet place.

	PETRIE
	Why, we'd be—
TOGETHER	MARION
	Oh, no, not at this time. Thank you.

The group has moved almost to the door—CAMERA PANNING
WITH THEM.

SCHUYLER
(to Marion)
I want you to understand that everything is being
done for him.

PETRIE
Oh, we realize that, Monsieur.

Schuyler and Victoria now go out. CAMERA CLOSES UP ON
MARION.

MARION
(her voice trembling with hatred)
Everything being done for him, everything. He
killed my sister, but everything is being done because he's rich. Everything! Oh, my God!

Petrie is trying to put his arms around her to comfort her.

DISSOLVE TO:

121. ESTABLISHING SHOT OF RITZ HOTEL IN PARIS
122. AN UPPER CORRIDOR OF THE RITZ
Outside the entrance to a magnificent suite. A pageboy is
approaching the suite with a small package; at the same
time a waiter is coming out carrying a tray with empty
dishes, empty bottles of wine, etc. They exchange expres-
sive glances which seem to say "How is he, this rich
American?"—"Oh, about the same." The waiter holds up
a hundred-franc note that he has received as a tip and
raises his eyebrows.

CAMERA GOES THROUGH the door with the pageboy. We are in
the anteroom of the suite, in itself a foyer that would be
impressive in a mansion. (Description follows.)

In the anteroom at present are two doctors. Dr. Benoit, the
outgoing one, is unimportant to our story. The other is Dr.

86

Franciscus, goat-bearded and of an Oriental and somewhat sinister aspect. Their bags repose on a table.

PAGEBOY
From the drugstore, Messieurs.
He leaves it on the table, looks cynically at the two doc-
tors, and goes out.

DR. BENOIT
(rather stiffly)
Perhaps you can do better than I, Dr. Franciscus.

DR. FRANCISCUS
(politely)
Mr. Schuyler seemed to feel that a change of treat-
ment—

DR. BENOIT
(interrupting impatiently)
As you wish. The Americans like dozens of doctors.

DR. FRANCISCUS
Perhaps to distribute the money more equitably.

DR. BENOIT
(bristling)
I assure you, sir, my charges have been moderate.

DR. FRANCISCUS
(also bristling)
Sir.

DR. BENOIT
(stiffly)
Your servant, sir.

DESCRIPTION OF SUITE:
It should consist of the aforesaid anteroom and a huge
salon opening out from it through double doors which are

at present closed, and of two bedrooms and two baths that open to both the anteroom and the salon. One of these bedrooms is important to later action, the other needs merely to be indicated by a door. There are many such suites in the Paris hotels intended for visiting royalty or for multimillionaires. The set designer can go overboard on the thing without danger.

In a salon as large as this, there would be several "centers." In this one there must be at least two. A group of chairs, table, couch, etc., near the French windows and another furniture grouping near the anteroom door, perhaps around a fireplace, naturally not in use in July. This arrangement is necessary for the sake of certain scenes, and will be referred to as "near the window" or "near the fireplace."

He goes brusquely past Dr. Franciscus and out. Franciscus looks after him malevolently, then looks at the double doors. As he approaches them, we hear a low murmur of voices, a man and a woman. Franciscus seems to be waiting for someone before he goes in. He'd like to know a little more about the situation. But whoever he's waiting for hasn't come. He knocks. After a moment:

WOMAN'S VOICE

Who is it, please?

DR. FRANCISCUS

Dr. Franciscus.

At this, the two double doors open automatically and we are looking lengthwise into the great salon. In the foreground is a stout, husky, white-capped American nurse who has just pressed the buttons opening the doors. At the far end of the salon seventy feet away we see against the triple French windows, the figure of Charles Wales in a bathrobe, his face unshaven, his hair unbrushed. He is passing slowly in front of the French windows, not interested in who is at the door. The doctor goes in. The doors close slowly behind him.

Now the door from the outer hall is opened by a valet-de-chambre who admits Dwight Schuyler and Victoria. Victoria is frightened and eager. Valet-de-chambre goes out of shot.

SCHUYLER

> I'll just go in first and find out if your father can see you now.

He knocks at the salon door. Meanwhile, Victoria sits down on a high-backed chair. The big double doors open, Schuyler goes in, and the doors close after him. Door from the outer hall opens again and the same valet-de-chambre admits a new character. This is Julia Burns, who is to be important in the story. She is a nurse, but not in white. She carries a small bag.

Victoria and Julia look at each other.

JULIA

> *(politely)*
> Good morning.

VICTORIA

> Good morning.

Julia Burns sits down at the opposite side of the anteroom. She is about twenty-six. It is not a beautiful face but distinctly a pretty one, with sometimes a certain sadness. It is important that the audience doesn't say at this point, "Here comes the love interest." Therefore, this girl's prettiness should not be the first thing that we notice about her, and this must be remembered in the casting. At present, she is *just a nurse.*

JULIA
> *(to Victoria after a pause)*
> Do you know if Dr. Franciscus is here?

VICTORIA
> No, I don't.

The door of the salon opens and Dr. Franciscus, without his bag, and Dwight Schuyler come out.

DR. FRANCISCUS
> Ah, this is the nurse I was telling you about.

SCHUYLER
> *(with bare politeness)*
> Oh, yes.

He nods. Julia stands up.

SCHUYLER
> *(to the doctor)*
> Perhaps we can talk in the hall.
> *(to Victoria)*
> Be with you in a minute, dear.

Dr. Franciscus and Schuyler go on out into the hall, closing the door behind them. Victoria notices a suitcase against the wall beside her. Idly she looks at the tag.
INSERT: TAG: HELEN WALES, NEW YORK.
Victoria stares into space a moment. Then drops the tag and regains her composure.

Julia lifts her head as there is the sound of a man's voice from the salon saying something indistinguishable. The sound dies away. Then she looks at Victoria.

JULIA

>Hadn't you better take off your coat?

VICTORIA

>>*(confidentially)*
>My dress is dirty. I came quick.

Julia smiles. Door from the outside hall opens, and Schuyler and Doctor come in.

SCHUYLER

>>*(to Victoria)*
>All right, dear, we'll go in now.

He knocks and in a moment the double doors open. Victoria and Schuyler start into the big room toward the figure at the end.

123. TWO SHOT—THE ANTEROOM—DR. FRANCISCUS AND JULIA

The shot includes the double doors closing. The doctor, after being sure the doors are closed, addresses Julia Burns.

DR. FRANCISCUS

>Well, Mrs. Burns,
>>*(significantly)*
>I'm giving you an—opportunity.
>>*(pause—her face is expressionless)*
>When a nurse hasn't worked for five years, it is not easy to find a position in Paris, Mrs. Burns.

JULIA

>*Miss* Burns, please, Doctor.

DR. FRANCISCUS

>>*(nodding)*
>Your name is your own. But the *case*—is mine.

> *(pause—speaks with great significance)*
> It can last—as long as we want it to last, Mrs.—Miss
> Burns.

HOLD on them staring at each other for a minute.

124. THE BIG SALON—GROUP SHOT NEAR THE WIN-
DOW

Charles Wales sitting, the Stout Nurse standing beside him.
Schuyler stands beside Victoria. Wales's face is twitching
nervously. There is a bottle on the table in front of him
from which he presently pours himself a small drink.

SCHUYLER

> *(unusually jovial)*
> Victoria thought she'd like to have a look at you.

WALES

> *(to Schuyler)*
> You took a lot on yourself.

With difficulty, he masters his nerves and turns to Victoria.

WALES

> *(speaking gruffly)*
> How are you, dear? I've thought a lot about you.
> Haven't been very well.

He starts to run his hands through his hair.

WALES

> *(to stout nurse)*
> Bring me a comb.

As the Nurse turns away, he calls after her impatiently.

WALES

> I asked for the barber.

STOUT NURSE
(firmly, as she starts away again)
It was time for your rest, Mr. Wales.

It is suggested that the rest of this shot is photographed either from an angle that leaves out Victoria or that her back is to the Camera and she is standing very still. She would take this bravely with her chin up and her face showing as little emotion as possible.

WALES
Rest, rest. What's all this about rest? Is it something you take like a pill? I don't want to rest. I want to do something and go somewhere. Do you think that just *lying down* makes you sleep? These doctors and nurses seem to believe that all you have to do is say "rest," and immediately sweet sleep comes. My Heaven! They've given me every pill in their bags, and the miracle just doesn't happen. I want to get out of here. I'm going to Italy this afternoon.

Stout Nurse back in shot with comb and brush.

WALES
(continuing)
I want you to help me get dressed. I want to get out of here.

SCHUYLER
You're in no shape to travel, Charles. Dr. Franciscus thinks you ought to lay up right here and pull yourself together.

NURSE
(with brush)
Lean over, Mr. Wales, that's a good boy.

He starts to lean over, and she makes a pass at his hair, whereupon he grabs the brush and comb, goes to a side mirror, and begins to brush and comb it furiously himself.

WALES

> I want a chasseur to pack my bags. I'm going down to Italy—Greece, maybe.

He drops the brush on the floor and covers his face with his hands.

WALES

> No, not Italy, not Italy, not ever again Italy. Greece, though. Tell the porter to come up, the head porter.

125. TWO SHOT—SCHUYLER AND VICTORIA
Victoria has never seen her father like this and is naturally shocked. Schuyler helps this impression along by shaking his head sadly. However, during this whole scene, her attitude should never be intrusive. Whatever may be her reaction—sympathy, pity with perhaps a touch of shame— she does not display it.

VICTORIA

> *(rather timidly)*
> Perhaps you'd better rest, Daddy.

WALES

> *(to Victoria—not rudely)*
> What do you know about it?

He looks at her. An overwhelming wave of pity goes over him as he realizes that she, too, has suffered this loss. For a moment it seems to him that perhaps their destinies should lie together now. His thought is to take her with him, and for an instant there is a gleam of hope in his eye. He takes a step toward her, then the hope fades.

WALES

No, you've got to stay here. I couldn't take you with me. What good would *I* be to *you?* Do they treat you well over there?

(to Schuyler)

See that she has everything necessary. I mean clothes. I mean everything. Give Petrie something—five, ten thousand dollars. Send them all to Brittany this summer. Concarneau. Oh, no! Not to Concarneau!

(he controls himself)

Listen, child, anywhere you want, you go for the summer. Take them with you—your aunt, your uncle, your cousin. Understand? Be happy.

(looks at her closely)

Hold yourself up, don't you remember what I told you?

(pause)

VICTORIA

(with an effort)

You said like a queen.

WALES

(to Schuyler)

Get her out of here. Excuse me—not yet.

Covers his face with his hands again. Then continues:

WALES

Listen, child, I'll try and come to see you wherever you are. I'll be all right—soon. I got a little—cold when I got to Paris and it's pulled me down.

—pours himself a glass of whiskey.

WALES
> (as he tries, unsuccessfully, to smile at Victoria)
> They got me a doctor and a nurse, so everything is
> going to be all right.
> (sitting down, he repeats as if to himself)
> Everything.

Seeing him sitting down, the Stout Nurse tries again to
brush his hair. He pays no attention.

STOUT NURSE
> Now, you'll take that pill, won't you? With your little
> daughter here? I know she'd like you to take it if it
> will make you feel better.

He looks at the pill, which lies on the table with a glass of
water. He picks up the pill in one hand and the glass of
water in the other. He holds up the pill, laughing at it
bitterly.

WALES
> This cure *that*? Life cracks to pieces and you take a
> pill!

He crushes the pill between his fingers and flings the glass
of water at the floor. It is nowhere near Victoria, but she
steps back, as do Schuyler and the nurse, to be away from
the spray of water.

STOUT NURSE
> Now, Mr. Wales.

Wales's eyes fall on Victoria.

WALES
> I'm sorry. I didn't mean to frighten you.
> (to Schuyler, savagely)
> Why did you bring her here? Take her out!

He takes a step forward and accidentally upsets a table beside him, which falls in the direction of Victoria. This is entirely accidental but the effect as interpreted by those present, *though not by the audience,* is that he intended to push the table at Victoria.

126. NEW ANGLE—INCLUDING SAME GROUP
—and showing that Dr. Franciscus has come into the room and witnessed the scene.

WALES

>I oughtn't to see her. I didn't want to see her. She just reminds me and reminds me. If she turns her head sideways, it's *her* head; if she turns her face sideways, it's *her* face; if she turns her chin, it's *her* chin; if she moves her hand—did you bring her here for that?
>
>>*(to Dr. Franciscus)*
>
>—fools!

During this speech, Victoria has turned her head away. Her mouth is very set.

DR. FRANCISCUS

>>*(advancing toward him)*
>Yes, Monsieur Wales, yes, Monsieur Wales.
>>*(to Schuyler)*
>You'd better get the little girl out of here.

WALES

>>*(beside himself, speaking to Schuyler)*
>Don't do it again, do you hear? Don't do it again.

127. ANOTHER ANGLE
—leaving out Schuyler and Victoria, who presumably start out.

DR. FRANCISCUS
> *(to Stout Nurse)*
> You are off this case now, nurse. I've made other arrangements. Miss Burns is putting on her uniform. Leave me your chart, please, and collect your wages at the desk.

STOUT NURSE
> *(rather shocked)*
> I'm off?

Dr. Franciscus nods.

STOUT NURSE
> *(still somewhat shocked)*
> I'll get my chart.

She walks out of shot. Wales has listened to this without interest.

128. ANOTHER ANGLE—INCLUDING ONLY WALES AND DR. FRANCISCUS
—who sits down across from him.

DR. FRANCISCUS
> Mr. Wales, you're taking things too hard today. Remember—the prescription for shattered nerves is rest.

Wales looks up at him contemptuously, but doesn't answer.

DR. FRANCISCUS
> *(continuing)*
> You are not the first man from Wall Street who's broken down. And a cure takes time. Then, after two or three months, you go back and make another fortune—as good as ever.

He laughs as if he had told a joke.

WALES
Don't ever mention Wall Street to me.

129. ANOTHER ANGLE—SCHUYLER
—coming back alone from the anteroom into the salon.
He has overheard this last.

SCHUYLER
                    (To Franciscus)
Business is out, Doctor.
                    (to Wales)
This man is going to put you on your feet, old boy.

Wales doesn't answer. Then:

WALES
I didn't mean to upset that table.

SCHUYLER
That's *noth*ing. We all do things.

WALES
Let Marion take care of her.

DR. FRANCISCUS
          (nods significantly to Schuyler)
We're going to get your mind off yourself and your
immediate family. What are your hobbies, Mr.
Wales, besides business, I mean? What interests
you?

Pause.

WALES
Well—since you ask—death.

130. ANTEROOM—VICTORIA AND JULIA BURNS

They are sitting opposite each other in the same position they were in before, only now Victoria's face is tense and drawn. Julia has changed to her white nurse's uniform. She is looking with quiet interest at Victoria. The Stout Nurse comes out of one of the bedrooms into the anteroom. She has on a light coat over her nurse's uniform and carries a bag.

131. CLOSE SHOT—THE TWO NURSES

STOUT NURSE
> Well, good luck to you.

JULIA
> > *(inquiringly)*
> Hard going?

STOUT NURSE
> I've had worse. He's a nice man. I'm sorry to lose the case.

Julia Burns is noncommittal.

132. FULL SHOT—THE ANTEROOM

Victoria watching the two nurses but without much interest. Stout Nurse turns toward the door.

STOUT NURSE
> > *(pleasantly to Victoria)*
> Good-bye.

She goes out. Silence for a moment.

JULIA
> > *(to Victoria)*
> Mr. Wales is your father, isn't he?

VICTORIA
Yes.

>   *(after a moment)*
> I want to say good-bye to him—because he said he
> was going to go away somewhere.

JULIA
> All right.

Double doors open. Dr. Franciscus puts his head out.

DR. FRANCISCUS
> Miss Burns.

Julia goes into the salon and out of shot—passing Schuyler
and Dr. Franciscus, who are coming out into the anteroom.

DR. FRANCISCUS
> I shall remain awhile. I want to see if the injection
> takes effect.

SCHUYLER
>   *(indicating Victoria—who is lost in her own thoughts)*
> There is a delicate problem here. I think the aunt
> would like—

VICTORIA
> Mr. Schuyler, can I say good-bye to Daddy?

SCHUYLER
> But you did, dear.

VICTORIA
> That wasn't good-bye. That wasn't anything at all.

Schuyler and Dr. Franciscus exchange a glance.

DR. FRANCISCUS
Under the circumstances—

SCHUYLER
(interrupting)
Your father is resting now, dear.

Victoria goes stubbornly to the door and knocks on it. Schuyler takes a step toward her but too late. The doors have opened.

133. NEW ANGLE
shooting at Victoria from inside the salon. She comes about ten feet into the room.

VICTORIA
Daddy! I just want to tell you I'll do everything you said. Everything you had time to tell me on the boat. Everything, I'll do, Daddy. Don't ever worry.

134. MEDIUM TWO SHOT
—toward the window, including Julia Burns and Charles Wales. Julia is standing over him, her arms folded tentatively. Wales is looking in Victoria's direction. HOLD on this a moment, FAVORING JULIA'S FACE. She is terribly moved and disturbed by what the child has said.

135. GROUP SHOT BY DOOR
Schuyler pulling Victoria back. Victoria waving with one hand.

136. TWO SHOT—WALES AND JULIA, FAVORING JULIA
Julia looks at the patient, then toward the child and then, instinctively, her hand rises and a smile comes onto her face as she waves at Victoria.

137. ANTEROOM
—Victoria, Schuyler, Dr. Franciscus coming out. The doors to the salon are closing.

VICTORIA
> *(getting herself in control)*
> I had to say good-bye. I'm all right now.

138. OUTER HALL
—Victoria and Schuyler coming out. As they start along the corridor, they pass waiters carrying dishes, a *femme de chambre* coming out of a room, etc. Victoria goes past them all, carrying herself like a queen.

FADE OUT

FADE IN:

139. A day has passed. Before the scene is fully lighted, we hear a man's voice reading in French. But as we only hear a part of this and it is in French, we do not yet know the purpose of what is going on.

As the SCENE LIGHTENS, we are looking at a SHEAF OF PAPERS held in a pair of masculine hands. A page is turned and the reading continues. CAMERA MOVES UP to show a face we have never seen before, that of a French lawyer. CAMERA PULLS BACK enough to indicate that we are in a bedroom, perhaps showing the foot of the bed, edge of a white sheet, etc.

140. CLOSE SHOT—MARION PETRIE
Her face hard, set, determined. The reading comes to an end and we hear the rustle of the papers offscene.

141. CLOSE SHOT—DWIGHT SCHUYLER

SCHUYLER
> Mr. Wales understands, I'm sure.

142. CLOSE SHOT—DR. FRANCISCUS
His eyes narrow and canny.

SCHUYLER'S VOICE
> *(continuing, offscene)*
> —don't you, old boy. It's just what you wanted.

143. CLOSE SHOT—THE LAWYER

The papers are in the shot and he has a fountain pen in his hand. He is leaning over what is obviously a bed.

LAWYER
(with French accent)
You understand that you are giving the guardianship of your daughter to her aunt and uncle, Monsieur and Madame Pierre Petrie, until her majority. Together with a trust fund that provides for her care.

144. CLOSE TWO SHOT—SCHUYLER AND PETRIE

SCHUYLER
(looking at his watch)
My boat-train leaves in an hour. We'll see Charles through, won't we.

CAMERA FAVORS PETRIE, grieved and solemn. CAMERA MOVES SWIFTLY from Schuyler and Petrie to a CLOSE SHOT OF JULIA. This PAN should show that she is standing further back from the bed and not in sight of anyone else, an expression of deep concern in her face. CAMERA PANS FORWARD WITH HER as she comes to arrange pillows so he can sign and we almost fancy that her head shakes from side to side as if saying "Don't do it." (We do not see Charles Wales's face.)

WALES'S VOICE
(offscene; sleepy, half drugged, very low)
Anything you decide. Anything.

SCHUYLER'S VOICE
(offscene; very kindly)
It seems best to everyone, Charles. You'll have no responsibilities.

Silence; sound of a pen scratching.

145. BLURRED SHOTS OF ALL SIX FACES
as they might appear to Charles Wales lying on the bed.

WALES'S VOICE
(over shot)
Now let me sleep.

The faces draw off from him suddenly and blur into a gray
distance, as we

FADE OUT

SEQUENCE D

FADE IN:

146–153. A MONTAGE—showing the passage of Victoria's summer in a seaside town (Concarneau in Brittany).

(a) Victoria and Richard netting for crabs at low water; (b) The Petries with Victoria and Richard and some other children, climbing old ruins; (c) Petrie and Richard tossing a ball on the beach in swimming costume. Petrie's costume is a little old-fashioned but not ludicrous. They wear straw peasant hats; (d) Victoria on a floating platform, trying to get a swimming fat man out of her way so she can dive from a six-foot board. She dives; (e) Victoria writing in a wet bathing suit; (f) Letters addressed to Miss Julia Burns, c/o Mr. Charles Wales, Ritz Hotel, Paris; (g) School bells ringing; (h) Girls Victoria's age entering school gate in Paris.

154. A FRENCH NEWSPAPER (*Le Petite Parisienne*) held in a man's hand. Date does not show. Headlines are:

LES AVANCES SUR BOURSE SONT NORMALES, ON DIT
DOUZE MILLES HOMMES DE $1,000,000 EN ETATS-UNIS.

MARKET GAINS NORMAL? SAY PUNDITS
TWELVE THOUSAND NEW MILLIONAIRES IN AMERICA

CAMERA PULLS BACK to show that the paper is in the hands of Pierre Petrie. He reads with envious eyes—and signs. His clothes are a little newer than when we last saw him—and he has abandoned his rolled-up umbrella for a silver-headed cane like Schuyler's.

CAMERA CONTINUES TO PULL BACK—disclosing that he has stopped at a newspaper kiosk on a business street.

VICTORIA
>*(to Richard)*
>I wanted to take Daddy some cuff-buttons but they cost two hundred francs.

Richard is impressed at the amount. As they start down the street, CAMERA TRUCKING IN FRONT OF THEM, Petrie is dreaming of millionaires.

RICHARD
>Where do we have lunch, Papa?

VICTORIA
>Do we *have* to have lunch?

Richard glares. Even Petrie is shocked.

PETRIE
>Mais oui, ma petite. First we have lunch—
>*(he ticks it off on his fingers)*
>—then we meet your aunt. *Then* I will take you to see your father.

Victoria sighs but is polite.

VICTORIA
    I haven't seen him for so long.

They are passing an American-French Brokerage House.
Many people going in and out. Sign over the door reads:

HARRIGAN—JOSSANNE BANKERS
Members New York Stock Exchange
Transactions de Bourse

Pierre stops walking and looks with awe and fascination at
the brokerage house.

PETRIE
    (with a faraway look)
    This is where they make their millions, those Ameri-
cans.

RICHARD
    Why don't *we* make millions?

PETRIE
    (sadly)
    It is the Americans who make millions.

RICHARD
    (looking at Victoria almost with respect)
    Could *she* make a million?

Petrie looks down at Victoria as if she, too, were suddenly
a banker. A light comes into Victoria's eyes.

VICTORIA
    Is it like baccarat at the Casino?

PETRIE
    (nodding)
    Exactly. You bet your money.

Victoria opens her purse and extracts a folded hundred-franc note.

VICTORIA
> Maybe I could make enough to buy the cuff-buttons—

Petrie gets the idea. He is shocked—he starts to hurry them along.

RICHARD
> *(catching his hand)*
> But Papa, *I* have fifty francs saved up.

Two Americans come out of the Banking House and into scene.

1st AMERICAN
> Ten million shares traded already!

Second American leans against the doorpost taking a *New York Herald* (Paris Edition) out of his pocket. First American goes out of shot. CAMERA FAVORS PETRIE, who has never been so tempted in his life. His hand goes instinctively to his breast pocket—we guess he has money on him.

VICTORIA
> Let's go in, Uncle Pierre.

RICHARD
> *(purse in hand)*
> Papa, look, I can make this into one hundred, one thousand francs, can't I?

PETRIE
> *(wavering)*
> Oh, mon Dieu!

> (to Victoria)
> Do you know anything about the stock market?
> (coming to himself)
> But no.

RICHARD
> (guessing his father's thoughts)
> I'd never tell Maman, mon pere. I would hide the winnings under my mattress.

Petrie takes out his purse, looks at his money, then at brokerage house.

PETRIE
> (aloud, to himself)
> Decision, that is what the Americans have. Decision!

He takes the children's hands firmly and walks toward the fatal doors. CAMERA REMAINS upon Second American. It CLOSES up to the dateline of the *Paris Herald*. THURSDAY, OCTOBER 29, 1929. Hold on the dateline—large letters. Over it the sound of a stock ticker.

155. CLOSE SHOT—TICKER TAPE
Reading: STOCKS CRASH FORTY POINTS.

156. A STOCK BOARD
With four boys working on it frantically. Over shot comes a moaning sound, as if from a hundred voices. CAMERA MOVES UP to a clock whose hands turn quickly from one o'clock to one thirty.

157. EXT. STREET IN FRONT OF BROKERAGE HOUSE
Petrie and children coming out. The children are shocked and alarmed, Petrie is wild-eyed. Obviously, they have lost everything in their pockets at one turn of the wheel.

PETRIE
> (to Richard)
> If you ever mention this to your mother—

VICTORIA
  What happened, Uncle Pierre? Did we lose?

PETRIE
  Now I understand how they get their money!

RICHARD
          (anxiously)
  Can we still have lunch, Papa?

PETRIE
          (feeling in his empty pockets)
  Lunch, Lunch! And if you mention to your Maman
  that we didn't have lunch—

As the three start off scene in a chastened mood,
                                    DISSOLVE TO:
158. EXT. MOTO-FRANCE TRAVEL AGENCY, PARIS
Petrie and the two children going in.
159. INT. MOTO-FRANCE TRAVEL AGENCY
The main room of the agency is cut in two by a long desk
with a mail department on one side and a touring bureau
on the other. There are easy chairs around for clients to
read their mail in, etc. Pierre Petrie is assistant manager.
Pierre and the children come in from the street.

PETRIE
          (to woman mail clerk)
  Has my wife come?

MAIL CLERK
  She's in the office, Monsieur Petrie.

PETRIE
          (to the children)
  Wait here, and—
          (he puts his finger to his lips)

—as he starts alone toward the rear of the agency.

160. PRIVATE OFFICE—MARION PETRIE AND NICHOL-
SON (Petrie's boss)

Nicholson is an American, probably a $10,000-a-year man. There is a safe in this shot.

NICHOLSON

Madame Petrie, Americans have spent one hundred million here this summer.

Marion is polite but not interested. She is thinking distastefully of the meeting between Victoria and her father this afternoon.

NICHOLSON (cont.)

We Americans have a gift for money making, Madame Petrie. I have a few nice things myself.
(he touches the safe significantly)
A banker friend told me to—just put 'em away and forget about 'em.

Petrie comes in. He feels so guilty that he can hardly face his wife. Nicholson bows to Marion and exits.

MARION
(absently)
Did you have a nice luncheon?

PETRIE
(startled)
Luncheon?

MARION
What did you give them?

PETRIE
(vague)
Oh, American Can, Chicago Wheat—
(stops himself)

112

MARION
>   *(puzzled)*
> Not fresh vegetables?

PETRIE
> It is time to take Victoria to her father.

Pause. Marion's eyes narrow.

MARION
> I have just talked to—to Miss *Burns* on the tele-
> phone. I told her the child is not to be left alone in
> the room with her father.
>   *(in a voice of protest)*
> Why couldn't we have just gone on—like the last
> three months? Victoria's been happy—she hardly
> mentions her father to me.
>   *(almost angrily)*
> I don't trust that nurse! If Charles is ranting and
> raving, don't stay one minute!

PETRIE
>   *(nervously)*
> Oui, oui, oui.

MARION
>   *(again absently)*
> Will you take a bus or a taxi?

PETRIE
>   *(who hasn't a cent)*
> It's such a lovely day, we shall probably walk.

They start out of the private office.
161. STREET OUTSIDE
Dwight Schuyler getting out of a taxi. There is a deep

change in him. For a moment he looks like a man in the grip of deadly fear.

162. ANOTHER ANGLE—EXT. TRAVEL AGENCY

Marion and Richard come out as Schuyler approaches the door. They do not see him, nor he them.

163. INT. LOBBY OF TRAVEL AGENCY

Schuyler coming in. CAMERA FOLLOWS HIM past Victoria, who is sitting rather restlessly in a big leather chair. She looks up, recognizing him, but doesn't hail him.

SCHUYLER
(to clerk at desk)
Mr. Petrie, please.

WIDER ANGLE SHOWS PETRIE, who has just started back toward the private office. He hears his name, turns and comes to the desk, shaking hands with Schuyler.

SCHUYLER
Just off the boat, Monsieur Petrie.

PETRIE
(surprised)
Well, Mr. Schuyler!

They walk back toward the office.

PETRIE (cont.)
Today, I'm taking the little one to see her father.

164. THE MAIL DEPARTMENT—VICTORIA WALKING UP

WOMAN CLERK
(pleasantly)
You expect some mail?

114

VICTORIA
> *(cheerfully)*
> Oh, no, I never get any mail. There was a girl who used to write me, but she stopped. I'm practically French now.

A little French messenger boy comes into shot and drops a stack of cables on the mail counter.

MESSENGER BOY
> Something in Wall Street. Mon Dieu, I'm giving batches like this to every bank in Paris.

The clerk starts to put them in their pigeonholes. The little messenger boy winks at Victoria, who doesn't respond.

MESSENGER BOY
> Hm-m- American? Jolie femme!

165. PETRIE'S OFFICE
Schuyler has spread some papers before Petrie.

SCHUYLER
> You merely authorize us to reinvest the child's money as the market changes. Things happen so fast that it's our duty to the child to increase her profits.

PETRIE
> But today the market—

SCHUYLER
> *(firmly)*
> It's up again. That's just the sort of thing we run into.

PETRIE
> But Madame Petrie—

SCHUYLER
> Women don't understand finance, do they? I think
> we'll be able—
>> *(Petrie has the pen in hand)*
> —to give you and Madame Petrie an even larger
> allowance for Victoria's care. It is exactly as her fa-
> ther wished.

Petrie still hesitates. There is a knock at the door. Schuyler
looks annoyed, Petrie relieved, as Victoria puts her head
in.

VICTORIA
> Hello, Mr. Schuyler.

SCHUYLER
> Hello, Victoria.

VICTORIA
>> *(to her uncle)*
> We won't have much time with Daddy.

Pierre, even more relieved, turns to his hat and coat.
Schuyler gathers up the papers.

SCHUYLER
>> *(to Victoria with a forced smile)*
> You're seeing your father?

They start out.

166. THE MAIL DESK

Another messenger boy is unloading cables. Almost in-
stantly he is joined by a third boy with another batch.

167. ANOTHER ANGLE—SHOWING SCHUYLER, PETRIE,
AND VICTORIA

Passing the mail desk on their way out, not noticing the
cables. CAMERA REMAINS ON MAIL DESK. Nicholson, the man-

ager, comes into shot. Several worried clients are opening
cables at mail desk.

MAIL CLERK
(confidentially, to Nicholson, holding up cables)
Over a hundred—all about the market.

NICHOLSON
(smiling complacently)
I get *my* advice from a man in the *know*. Then I put
'em away and—

He reads over a client's shoulder, does a "Takem" and
returns to the clerk in sudden alarm.
168. SIDEWALK CAFE—A TABLE—WAITING TAXI IN
B.G.
Petrie and Schuyler; Victoria is standing up, trying not to
look impatient. The papers are again spread before Petrie.
The two men have small beers.

SCHUYLER
You know, Petrie, you always struck me as more
American than French. You have—decision.

Petrie flinches at the word—nevertheless, the flattery re-
stores his confidence.

SCHUYLER (cont.)
A Frenchman would take hours to understand a deal
like this—red tape—formality.
Petrie picks up his pen, hesitates again.

PETRIE
Could you advance me ten francs until tomorrow?

SCHUYLER
Certainly! Here's a hundred.

117

Petrie hesitates once more. Maybe signing this paper will recoup his little loss of today. He signs.

PETRIE
Voilà! Are you coming with us to see Charles?

SCHUYLER
(concealing his satisfaction)
No.
(to Victoria)
I want to surprise your father—so don't tell him I'm in Paris.

CAMERA PANS with Victoria and Petrie toward the taxi.

VICTORIA
(to taxi man)
Vite! S'il vous plaît.

169. PHONE BOOTH IN THE CAFÉ—DWIGHT SCHUY-LER

SCHUYLER
Dr. Franciscus? Dwight Schuyler speaking . . .
(deliberately)
I was surprised to learn that Mr. Wales is well enough to see his daughter.
(evidently the doctor protests his ignorance of the matter—Schuyler's face is impatient)
If you go there don't tell him I'm in town. I'm very busy . . . Yes, naturally the market.

Schuyler hangs up, wiping his head with handkerchief. He looks in his pocket to see if the document is safely there, and starts out.

170. CORRIDOR OF THE RITZ—OUTSIDE CHARLES WALES'S DOOR

CAMERA CLOSES UP to sign

DO NOT DISTURB

DISSOLVE TO:

171. FULL SHOT—WALES'S SALON EMPTY

DISSOLVE TO:

172. CHARLES WALES'S BEDROOM

Julia Burns standing beside a chest of drawers. She is looking o.s. with amusement. Bed is not in shot.

WALES'S PLEASANT VOICE
> *(offscene)*
> Why don't you sometimes wear something—more personal. I mean something green or pink, or a hat with a bird on it.

JULIA
> Not in style.

WALES
> Sure they are. My mother always used to have a bird in her hat. Once my brother and I cut a couple of birds off her hat and put them in a cage with a canary.

173. WIDE-ANGLE SHOT—WALES

Wales at the bureau, dressed and fixing his collar and tie.

WALES (cont.)
> Afterwards when the canary died, we sewed it on one of her hats and she was wild.

While Wales is not the vital, world-conquering man whom we saw in New York, he has come a long way back in the past three months. He is quiet, seems several years older—but some humor has crept back into his face.

119

The bedroom phone clicks, and Julia picks it up.

JULIA
>> (into phone)
>> Send them up and ask them to please wait in the anteroom.

WALES
>> Is that Victoria?
>> (a certain fear comes into his face)
>> This may be a mistake.

JULIA
>> It's not a mistake, Mr. Wales. It's a step forward, and it's time for you to take it.
>> (she hesitates)
>> Another thing. I'm leaving you, Mr. Wales. I'm going back to America.

Wales takes it big.

WALES
>> You're what?

JULIA
>> The case is finished.

WALES
>> When are you going to America?

JULIA
>> Next week. But I'm leaving today.
>> (smiles)
>> I don't think I care to face Dr. Franciscus. He doesn't know that you've ever been dressed.

WALES
>
> (with mock gravity)
> Oh, it's time for my sleeping potion.

He takes a half-empty bottle of pills from the dresser and carefully drops three into the waste basket.

JULIA
>
> I've been very unprofessional—encouraging you to get out and take walks and—

Wales has finished his collar and tie. He stands up and walks a few paces.

WALES
>
> Well, I suppose you had to leave sooner or later, but it makes me feel helpless in a cold world.
> (turns to her)
> You pulled me through this.

He walks to bureau drawer and looks for a handkerchief.

JULIA
>
> (thoughtfully)
> Well—I had Victoria to account to.

As they start toward the door to the living room,

DISSOLVE TO:

174. ANTEROOM OF THE SUITE
—Victoria sitting. Petrie and Dr. Franciscus standing and talking fast over Victoria's head. The American words come through startlingly.

DR. FRANCISCUS
>
> Les nouvelles de *New-York* sont formidables! J'ai acheté des *stocks* de *General Electric* aussi *A.T. and T.* et ce matin ils sont tombés jusqu'au fond. [The

news from N.Y. is terrible! I bought stock in General
Electric and A.T. and T. and this morning they've
fallen to nothing.]

PETRIE

> Oui! J'ai joué aux transactions de *Wall-Street*
> aujourd'hui. J'ai perdu sur *National Cash Register.*
> [Yes! I played the market on Wall Street today. I lost
> on National Cash Register.]

Julia opens the door to the Salon. Victoria shakes hands
with her shyly.

> > DR. FRANCISCUS
> > *(over shot)*
> > > Je ne sais pas si c'est une
> > > panique. [I do not know
> > > whether it is a panic.]

TOGETHER   PETRIE
> > *(over shot)*
> > > Je ne pense pas que c'est une
> > > panique. Mais on ne sait jamais
> > > à *Wall-Street.* [I do not think it
> > > is a panic but you never can tell
> > > on Wall Street.]

175. SALON—BY THE WINDOW—CLOSE SHOT CHARLES
     WALES IN AN ARMCHAIR

His expression is rigid, tense. He doesn't know whether
once again the contours of Victoria's face will remind him
of his dead wife. He makes an impatient gesture, then
steels himself as he hears:

VICTORIA'S VOICE
> > *(over shot)*
> Daddy!

Wales turns and faces them with a slow, difficult smile.

176. ANOTHER ANGLE

VICTORIA
      (running toward him)
    Oh, Daddy, Daddy, Daddy, Daddy, Dads, Dads, Dads!

She jumps up into his arms, struggling like a fish and pulls his head around by one ear and sets his cheek against hers.

WALES
    Why, you little fella, you.

177. BY THE FIREPLACE—FRANCISCUS AND PETRIE
—who start at the sight of Wales. Petrie, after a second, is pleasantly surprised. Franciscus is aghast.
178. BY THE WINDOW—ANOTHER ANGLE
Wales stands up and starts o.s. toward Petrie and Franciscus, holding out his hand. Victoria turns to Julia.

VICTORIA
      (overjoyed)
    You *wrote* me he was better!

JULIA
      (confidentially)
    He knows your letters by heart.

179. BY THE FIREPLACE—WALES, PETRIE, AND FRAN-CISCUS

PETRIE
      (with honest happiness)
    You are a new man, Charles. Dressed and all! I'm overwhelmed—*bouleversé.*

Wales turns to Franciscus.

WALES
    Monsieur le docteur—
        (politely but firmly)
    I think this is your farewell visit.

DR. FRANCISCUS
        (puzzled)
    You are leaving? For America?

WALES
    Not quite yet.

DR. FRANCISCUS
        (suddenly it seems plain to him)
    Ah, the stock market!

The men move toward the window, CAMERA PANNING WITH
THEM

WALES
        (shortly)
    I've quit the stock market.

PETRIE
    But today, Charles—

CAMERA FAVORS FRANCISCUS, who is suddenly afraid he may
never see his money.

DR. FRANCISCUS
    Would you mind if I presented my bill right away,
    Monsieur Wales.

WALES
    Present it at the desk, Dr. Franciscus.

Victoria and Julia are now included in the shot. Franciscus looks resentfully at Julia.

DR. FRANCISCUS
    And Mademoiselle Burns—

WALES
           (interrupting)
    At the desk, Dr. Franciscus!
           (pointedly)
    In the lobby.

CAMERA FAVORS FRANCISCUS

DR. FRANCISCUS
    (clenching his hands and looking at the ceiling)
    Ah, *gratitude!*

He turns and goes out of shot.

WALES
           (to Petrie)
    How's Marion—and the sprout?

Petrie stares at him uncomprehending.

WALES
    You know, the papoose?

Petrie shakes his head, still confounded.

VICTORIA
           (laughs)
    He means Reeshard, Uncle Pierre, He's teasing.

PETRIE
           (fascinated)
    Ah, you still call them papooses in America? *Still,* after all these years? C'est epouvantable!

VICTORIA
Daddy, what about that trip to the Cannibal Isles?

Wales looks at her. Traveling with her is a new idea to him. He doesn't know whether he likes it or not. But the child he likes. There is warmth in the way he's looking at her now. CAMERA FAVORS PETRIE.

PETRIE
(to Victoria, with some alarm)
You're at school now, you and Reeshard. In five years you have your baccalaureate examination.
(he now thinks she is Richard)
If you pass that well, you may not have to do your army service.

WALES
(amused)
Does she have to go in the army?

PETRIE
I was speaking of Reeshard. But Marion has made her plans for them both.

Wales takes this noncommittally. He looks at Victoria.

WALES
How's tricks—are you in love?

VICTORIA
Oh no, Daddy.

WALES
Do you like maple-banana-raspberry ice cream? Because I know where we can get some.

126

Petrie is at a loss. The lineup is so different from what he had expected that Marion's instructions seem academic. He starts to object, but Julia anticipates him.

JULIA

It'll be all right. I don't think Madame Petrie understood on the telephone.

PETRIE

(hopefully, to Julia)
You and I will accompany them.

JULIA

I must pack.

VICTORIA

Pack?
(to her father in alarm)
Who's going to take care of you?

JULIA

(to Victoria)
I think he can take care of himself.
(sees that Victoria is not quite convinced)
Tomorrow I'll look in and see.

PETRIE

(desperately)
But I should *love* this extraordinary ice cream. That is what you call a "gas station"?

WIPE DISSOLVE TO:

180. INT. RUMPELMAYER'S TEA SHOP—WALES AND VICTORIA

This was a fashionable rendezvous, specializing in ices, delicate sandwiches, etc. An orchestra would be playing "Blue Heaven" or "Among my Souvenirs." Victoria has a

large ice in front of her, Wales has coffee. The scene
should go very simply and quietly. Wales is trying to get to
know his daughter again, trying to enter her life. He talks
to her as to an adult—gravely, respectfully, without any
tremolo.

WALES
I'm glad you're doing so well at school.

VICTORIA
I'm third. Reeshard is only eighteenth.

WALES
You like Richard?

VICTORIA
Quite well.

WALES
(trying to draw her out about her life)
And Aunt Marion and Uncle Pierre? Which do you
like best?

VICTORIA
(thinking)
Oh, Uncle Pierre, I guess.
(pause)
She gets so excited.
(as if she had often thought of this)
Why don't I live with you? Because Mother's dead?

Pause.

WALES
But you're learning French.
(pause)
And it would have been hard for me to take care of
you.

128

VICTORIA

But I don't need taking care of, any more than you
do.

Pause.

WALES

(*slowly*)
Darling, do you ever think of your mother?

VICTORIA

Yes, sometimes.

WALES

I don't want you to ever forget her. Have you got a
picture of her?

VICTORIA

Aunt Marion has.

WALES

She loved you very much.

VICTORIA

I loved her too.
(*pause*)
Daddy, I want to come and live with you.

Sudden joy comes into Wales's face, but he controls it.

WALES

Aren't you happy?

VICTORIA

Yes, but I like you better than anybody—and you like
me better than anybody, don't you—now that
Mother's dead?

WALES

(this is a little difficult)

Of course. Of course, I do. But you won't always like me best, honey. You'll grow up and meet somebody your own age and go marry him, and forget you ever had a father.

VICTORIA

(tranquilly)

Yes, that's true.

He looks at her as she glances around the room. He has found her at last. It is apparent that he wants her with him now.

DISSOLVE TO:

181. EXT. PETRIE'S APARTMENT AT DUSK
Wales and Victoria getting out of taxi. Victoria has a box under her arm. PAN WITH THEM to archway shown in Sequence A. CAMERA MOVES AHEAD OF THEM to show Petrie leaning despondently on his cane in the Archway. He looks o.s., sees Wales and Victoria, and goes eagerly toward them, CAMERA PANNING WITH HIM.

PETRIE

(taking Victoria's hand—speaking timorously)

You must be tired, Charles.

WALES

(firmly)

I'd like to see Marion

182. INT. PETRIE'S LIVING ROOM
Marion looking at her wristwatch. Sound of door opening off-scene. Dismay comes into her face as she sees Wales entering the hall, then an expression of impersonal coldness.

183. ANOTHER ANGLE. WALES AND VICTORIA COMING IN

MARION
    Hello, Charles.

WALES
            (shyly cordial)
    Hello, Marion.

Marion casts a glance at Victoria as if to see if any damage has been done; then looks at Charles with what amounts to indignant surprise.

MARION
    I see you're feeling better.

WALES
            (nods)
    We had a great afternoon.

Victoria goes o.s.

PETRIE
        (after an uneasy glance at Marion)
    Charles, today the stock market—

WALES
            (interrupting)
    I'm out of the stock market, Pierre; I don't care what it does. It can't hurt us.

MARION
    No, not now!

The stab goes home to Wales.
184. ANOTHER PART OF THE LIVING ROOM

Richard is coming out of his room. Victoria is opening the
big box that she has brought in.

RICHARD
Qu'est-ce que c'est? [What's that?]

VICTORIA
For you, Reeshard.

She lifts out a big box of French soldiers.

RICHARD
Oh, Maman! Oh, Papa!

185. GROUP SHOT—MARION, PETRIE, AND WALES
Marion looks listlessly at the present, resenting that also.

WALES
(feeling his way)
I don't want to interfere with Victoria's life for the
present. I'd like her to stay on with you—but a little
later—

MARION
(very tense)
My duty is entirely to Helen. I try to think what she
would have wanted me to do.

She glances at the children and lowers her voice.

MARION (cont.)
Frankly, from—that—day you haven't really existed
for me, Charles. She was my sister.
Petrie puts his arm around Marion, trying to calm her.
Wales's face is growing hard and set.

132

WALES
   I'll say good night.

He turns and starts toward the door, turns back.

WALES
         (stubbornly)
   I'm not going to lose Victoria's childhood, Marion—
   you can understand that.

Marion doesn't answer. Petrie takes Wales's arm and CAM-
ERA PANS WITH WALES AND PETRIE into hall.

PETRIE
         (to Wales in a whisper)
   She is a little upset.

As Wales opens the door.
186. INT. LIVING ROOM
Richard is taking out the French soldiers and setting them
on the table, Victoria helping.

VICTORIA
   (looking up surprised, as she hears the doors closing)
   Did Daddy go?

Marion nods.

VICTORIA
   Can I go and see him tomorrow?

MARION
         (with an effort)
   I don't think so, dear.

VICTORIA
   But it's his birthday!

133

Marion turns away shaking her head. CAMERA FAVORS VICTO-RIA. Now she realizes for almost the first time that Marion doesn't want her to see her father.

DISSOLVE TO:

187. INT. RITZ HOTEL—WALES COMING IN FROM STREET

He slows down, remembering that the pleasant nurse is not waiting upstairs—a lonely dinner lies ahead. At the sound of raised voices o.s., he turns toward the men's bar.*

188. FULL SHOT RITZ BAR

The bar is jammed to the doors with the 7:30 crowd. At the many tables and leather corner seats there is only one overwhelming topic—the stock-market crash.

189. BY THE BAR—PAUL, THE FRENCH HEAD BAR-TENDER—WALES APPROACHING

WALES

    Hello, Paul.

PAUL

        (in perfect, civilized English)
    Why Mr. Charles Wales. I haven't seen you for years.
        (pantomimes "A drink?")

WALES

    Some Vichy.

PAUL

        (setting up a split of Vichy)
    Mr. Wales, what do you think of the market?
        (eagerly)
    My broker in New York wires me—

A MALE VOICE

        (singing strong suddenly o.s.)
    "Last night was the end of the wor-l-l-ld!"

* NOTE: Not to be confused with the Women's Bar, which was across a corridor.

PAUL
>   Excuse me one moment, Mr. Wales.

190. ANOTHER ANGLE
Showing other heads, two of which have turned at the
sound of Wales's name.

1st MAN (OTIS)
>   Why Charles!

WALES
>   Hello, Otis.

2nd MAN
> *(surprised)*
>   Well, Mr. Wales! You *seem* pretty cool.

OTIS
> *(to Wales)*
>   I'm meeting Dwight Schuyler here.

Wales is surprised that Schuyler is in town.

2nd MAN
> *(rather rudely)*
>   What's the lowdown—what are you fellows doing?
> *(stopping himself)*
>   Excuse me, Mr. Wales, but I've been watching that
>   ticker till I'm cuckoo.

The three men drink. There is a babble of voices consisting
mostly of the name of stocks. Paul back in Shot.

PAUL
>   Mr. Wales, have you a minute?

As Wales starts to turn, 2nd Man makes a grab at his lapel.

135

2nd MAN
> *(rude again)*
> Wait, Mr. Wales.

Wales brushes him off sharply and turns to Paul.

OTIS
> *(to 2nd Man in a lowered voice)*
> Let him alone, Jim. They're in up to their necks. Ball Brothers and Wales and Company *own* the finance trust.

WALES
> *(hearing, and turning slowly back)*
> What did you say? What finance trust?

191. BY THE DOOR
A Chasseur busy on telephone looks o.s. at the people coming in.

CHASSEUR
> Mr. Johnson—Mr. Schuyler.

CAMERA PANS TO DWIGHT SCHUYLER, who moves toward bar. Suddenly he sees Wales o.s. and stops dead.
192. BY THE BAR

2nd MAN
> *(to Wales)*
> Where have you been? China?

Realization has broken over Wales that his firm has apparently been ruined in the happenings of the day.

OTIS
> *(to 2nd Man)*
> Shut up. Charles has been sick.
> *(looks at his watch, wondering where Schuyler is)*

136

193. DWIGHT SCHUYLER
—turning away, starting quickly toward the door.

194. THE BAR

PAUL
> *(to Wales, whom he trusts)*
> Listen, Mr. Wales, you're one of the three—
> *(he holds up three fingers)*

Wales has been studying figures on an envelope that Otis has handed him. The figures dance before his eyes like fire.

2nd MAN
> Where have you been, that's what I want to know, China?

He looks for a laugh at Paul.

PAUL
> Mr. Wales is one of the three—
> *(he holds up three fingers and shakes them almost threateningly)*

SINGING VOICE
> *(o.s. sounds again)*
> "Last night was—

CAMERA PANS OFF TO SINGER, a fair-haired man of thirty with tears flowing down his cheeks.

SINGER
> "—the end of the wor-l-l-ld!"

CUT TO:

195. CHASSEUR WITH TELEPHONE—BY THE DOOR

CHASSEUR
>Mr. Bronson, Mr. Casey—Mr. Wales.

CAMERA PANS ASIDE to include Wales on his way out.

WALES
>*(to Chasseur)*
>If Mr. Schuyler comes in, ask him to call my suite upstairs.

As Wales starts out, the voice of the Singer sounds off once more.

>*DISSOLVE TO:*

196. CLOSE-UP: THE SIGN DO NOT DISTURB
—on door of Wales's suite. Wales's hand comes into shot taking it down. CAMERA PULLS BACK to show Wales opening door.

197. SUITE IN DARKNESS
—light goes on disclosing a table with two dozen cables piled on it.

Wales comes into shot, opens the first cable.

>*DISSOLVE TO:*

198. HALF HOUR LATER: SAME
—cables open and scattered on the table. Wales is handing two outgoing cables to the Bellboy.

WALES
>Send these.

Knocking o.s.

199. DOOR FROM THE ANTEROOM—THE HEAD POR-
>TER
He waits till Bellboy has gone out, shutting the door behind him. CAMERA PANS FORWARD WITH HIM, bringing Wales into shot.

HEAD PORTER

It will cost money, Monsieur Wales. There are only two radio phones between New York and Paris. If you want the entire use of one tomorrow—
(he shrugs his shoulders, implying the need of a sizable bribe)

WALES

(taking out his checkbook)
How much?

HEAD PORTER

Ten thousand francs, Monsieur.

WALES

The New York market is open by two P.M., Paris time. The connection must be installed before two.

Phone rings and he picks it up.

WALES

Hello. . . . Then try to find where Mr. Schuyler is *staying.* Try the Crillon, the Meurice, the Georges Cinq—

DISSOLVE TO:

200. DRAWING ROOM OF THE SUITE—1:30 P.M. NEXT DAY—GROUP SHOT

Wales in chair near the window. On the divan are Otis, Fat Broker, and Thin Broker, a bottle before them. Pageboy just leaving with cables. Bellboy on the telephone. Hotel Electrician coming out of Wales's bedroom.

BELLBOY

(into phone)
Oui.
(caps mouthpiece and turns to Wales)
Monsieur Schuyler is not at any hotel in Paris.

ELECTRICIAN
> *(to Wales)*
> The extension is now connected for New York, Monsieur.
> *(looks at his watch)*
> Your service will begin in seven and one-half minutes.

Wales nods.

WALES
> *(to Bellboy)*
> Never mind Mr. Schuyler. When the phone rings in my bedroom, pick it up and keep the line open.

CAMERA FAVORS the three men on the sofa.

FAT BROKER
> I could take this better in that little Wall Street speakeasy.

THIN BROKER
> Get on the boat with me tonight.

FAT BROKER
> It'll all be over by the time you get there.

OTIS
> How do you know?

FAT BROKER
> Oh, the president of Yale or Dartmouth or Bryn Mawr issued a statement. It was in the paper this morning. Said it can't last.

THIN BROKER
> What do they know about it? I'd like to hear what Morgan and Van Greff and those boys have to say.

FAT BROKER
>Anyhow—nobody's lost but the little guys—but the trouble is, I'm a little guy.

201. CORRIDOR OUTSIDE WALES'S SUITE
Victoria reaching her father's door. From her expression we guess that this is an unauthorized call. She carries a knitting bag, from a corner of which shows a folded paper. Another Pageboy with cables follows Victoria through the door.

202. GROUP BY THE WINDOW—INCLUDING BELL-BOY
Telephone shrills o.s. The three Brokers jump. Bellboy rushes o.s. in direction of bedroom.

203. NEAR DOOR OF ANTEROOM
CAMERA PANS Victoria and Pageboy through the long salon up to Wales.

WALES
>(surprised)
>Dear!

Pageboy leaves cables and goes o.s. Brokers stand up.

WALES
>My daughter, Mr. Otis—

204. BY THE BEDROOM DOOR
Bellboy re-entering.

BELLBOY
>(excitedly)
>They were trying the line.

Salon phone rings
205. GROUP SHOT

Brokers shaking hands with Victoria. Bellboy rushes into shot and takes up phone.

BELLBOY
> (to Wales, cupping receiver)
> Do you wish to have the river dragged for Mr. Schuyler?

Brokers start out.

OTIS
> (to Wales)
> If anybody can help Wales and Company, you can.

Wales shakes his head.

WALES
> Not blindfolded I can't. This is an operation with some funds of my own.

FAT BROKER
> (confidentially to Wales)
> Do you know what I think? I think Schuyler is keeping out of your way.

All three Brokers are now out of shot.

VICTORIA
> (to Wales, who is opening cables)
> Daddy, have you forgotten what day it is?

WALES
> Does your aunt know you're here, darling?

Without waiting for an answer he opens the first cablegram and frowns. Then, looking up, he doesn't notice she hasn't answered.

WALES
>Did you ask me what day it is?

VICTORIA
>>*(amused)*
>>Daddy, it's your birthday, October twenty-ninth.

WALES
>>*(touches her shoulder affectionately)*
>>Well, dear, I'm afraid we can't make a day of it.

Out of her bag Victoria fishes a few rows of knitting with needles. Wales opens more cablegrams.

VICTORIA
>>That's all right. I'm starting a sweater. Daddy, I brought you a poem I wrote.

She hands him a sheet of paper that he puts absently with the cablegrams.

WALES
>>Well, that's wonderful.

Telephone rings o.s. in bedroom. Bellboy comes into shot and goes o.s. to answer it.

WALES
>>*(looking up from cable)*
>>What's this about a poem?

VICTORIA
>>Oh, I just wrote it.

Wales opens another cable, reads it quickly, lifts his head as if memorizing it.

VICTORIA
> Will you read my poem after this one, Daddy?

206. BY THE DOOR OF BEDROOM—SHOOTING IN— BELLBOY ON PHONE

BELLBOY
> *(calling off)*
> It's New York, Monsieur Wales.

207. TWO SHOT—WALES AND VICTORIA

WALES
> *(calling off)*
> Hold it.
> *(to Victoria)*
> I'll read it right away.

He reads aloud. Victoria watches him tensely.

WALES
> *(reading)*
> "If he's sick upon his birthday
> You must tuck him safe in bed,
> Put the cake out of his sight
> Parents sick must not be fed.
>
> "Sometimes give him his medicine,
> It really doesn't taste bad.
> Mix it with some ice cream
> There, there, that's it, my lad."
> *(looks up and speaks admiringly)*
> That's *very* good.

208. DOOR OF BEDROOM—SHOOTING IN

BELLBOY
> *(into phone)*
> Just one minute—just one minute . . .

209. WALES AND VICTORIA

VICTORIA
> *(a little uneasy)*
> Daddy, is that the stock market?

Wales nods briefly.

VICTORIA
> *(thinking of her experience yesterday)*
> —because the stock market is awful. They take all
> your money. Uncle—
> *(she stops herself)*

Wales puts his hands affectionately on her shoulders.

WALES
> You sure you want to wait, dear?

Victoria nods determinedly. He nods and starts out.
210. THE BEDROOM
Wales comes into shot taking phone from boy, nodding for
him to go. Bellboy goes out. Wales sits on the bed.

WALES
> *(into phone)*
> Thank you, Genson? Look, I'm acting for my-
> self . . .
> *(dryly)*
> I thought I *had* quit, but Wall Street seems to be the
> road without an ending. Look, I want to distribute
> some business among three brokers, understand?
> . . . I want to sell some shares on a thirty-point mar-

gin. . . . Go out and borrow it and sell it. . . . I can cover it right away, three hundred fifty thousand dollars' worth of Liberty Bonds in the Gotham National. . . . Now, whatever happens don't hang up. I'm using code four . . .

211. WIDE-ANGLE SHOT—SALON
Victoria has begun knitting near the fireplace. Bellboy in a straight chair by the window.

212. BEDROOM
Wales on the phone. He shuts his eyes—he is talking from memory with intense concentration.

WALES
Through E 24, down to 120 steel 3. Forget the ticker. I hope I'm ahead of the ticker. E 1216—

DISSOLVE TO:

213. THE SAME—LATER
Wales is still at the phone. His hair is rumpled; he's taken off his tie; there is strain in his face.

WALES
(smiling faintly as he speaks into phone)
I told you two hours ago I was ahead of the ticker. Hold on, will you?
(calls o.s.)
Bellboy! Hold this phone.

214. EXT. RITZ HOTEL—SCHUYLER GETTING OUT OF TAXI
His cane clatters out of his hand and down on the sidewalk. But he's not drunk.

TAXI DRIVER
Les Americans nervous—eh?

146

215. WALES'S SALON—BY THE FIREPLACE

Victoria looking rather anxiously at her father, who has just come into the Salon. The sight of his face disturbs her; suddenly she is reminded of one of the days on the ship that culminated in her mother's tragedy. Intuition has made her not want to leave him. She has been foxy about it, quietly knitting. In b.g. through bedroom door we see the bellboy on phone.

BELLBOY
> Just one minute, please. . . .

VICTORIA
> *(sympathetically to her father)*
> Those bulls and bears must be pretty tired.

A knock o.s.

216. BY THE ANTEROOM DOOR—SCHUYLER COMING IN

SCHUYLER
> *(uneasy)*
> Hello, Charles—Victoria.

Wales looks grimly at Schuyler. Victoria stands up politely, then she sits down with an air of "Don't mind me" as Wales and Schuyler walk out of shot toward window.

WALES'S VOICE
> So you fellows were the big bankers, eh? Backing the wind!

Victoria has resumed her knitting and is paying no attention. The last sentence of Wales's speech is hardly audible, where she sits.

217. TWO SHOT—WALES AND SCHUYLER—BY THE WINDOW

SCHUYLER
　　Well, you quit us. You left us alone.
　　(as he pours himself a drink, his hand trembles)
　　You were sick, you couldn't think. Somebody had to.

WALES
　　　　　(with a short laugh)
　　Where have you been anyhow—hiding?

SCHUYLER
　　　　　(shakes his head)
　　I heard about the crash when I got to Paris yester-
　　day, and I've been trying to straighten things out.
　　Then I thought that if anybody could help salvage
　　something, it's Charles Wales.

Phone rings o.s. They pay no attention.

WALES
　　You're mad. I don't expect a penny on the dollar for
　　my money.

218. CHANGED ANGLE—WALES AND SCHUYLER
—showing Victoria putting down her knitting in b.g. and
advancing toward phone.

SCHUYLER
　　How about her money?

WALES
　　　　　(not getting it for a moment)
　　Her money?

Victoria has picked up phone.

SCHUYLER
　　Did you think we'd let it lie around at two and a half
　　percent?

WALES
>That money in the firm! Why, those investments were hog-tied, and you knew it!

VICTORIA
>Daddy!

She comes into shot looking a little guilty.

VICTORIA
>Daddy, would you represent me? It's Uncle Pierre.

Wales is so angry that it takes him a moment to get this; he goes o.s.

VICTORIA
>*(to Schuyler)*
>Do you like poetry, Mr. Schuyler?

Schuyler stares at her distractedly.
219. WALES AT PHONE
His temper is strained but he speaks quietly.

WALES
>Hello, Pierre.
>*(pause)*
>Yes. Listen, I want her to stay for dinner.
>*(pause)*
>No, she shouldn't have come without telling you. I realize that and I feel sorry that Marion is—
>*(pause)*
>No, I *insist* that she stay for dinner.
>*(pause; he speaks firmly)*
>Well, you calm Marion down.

220. TWO SHOT—SCHUYLER AND VICTORIA

VICTORIA
>*(reading from paper)*
>—"Mix it with some ice cream. There, there, that's it, my lad."

Wales comes into shot.

WALES
>Did you like it, Dwight?

SCHUYLER
>What? Oh, yes.

Victoria goes o.s., her expression saying "A mere trifle."

WALES
>You borrowed her money, Dwight. You ought to listen politely to her poem.

221. BY THE BEDROOM DOOR—VICTORIA AND BELL-BOY
He is saying "Just a minute, please" into phone, and mischievously she joins in.
222. WALES AND SCHUYLER

WALES
>Dwight, I've done you an injustice, I thought you were rather a lunk—you know—a respectable lunk. But what you are is a skunk. And just so nobody else will make a mistake, I'm going to dress you up in a nice new suit, with the stripes running—

He makes two circles with his forefinger, one above the other. Schuyler's hand travels to his tie.

WALES
>Leave it alone!

SCHUYLER
    What?

WALES
    Your tie. Leave it alone.

Schuyler leaves it alone.

SCHUYLER
    I rode with the times, Charles. You weren't there to
    help and you were all we had. That's why we insured
    your life for a million dollars—your brain! And then
    you quit.
        (he is breathing hard)
    There's nothing I can do. There isn't any million-
    dollar policy on my life.

223. CLOSE-UP—WALES
—who makes a contemptuous spitting sound.

WALES
    Don't worry, I'll jump out the window in a minute. I
    wouldn't want to have you not get your million,
    Dwight.

224. CLOSE-UP—SCHUYLER
The word *million* echoes in his head.
225. TWO SHOT—WALES AND SCHUYLER
Wales picks up Schuyler's silver-headed cane from the divan. Schuyler winces.

WALES
    Don't worry. I wouldn't touch you with a fish-pole.

He breaks the cane dispassionately over his knee and
hands the fragments to Schuyler.

WALES
> Your sword, Monsieur.

Schuyler doesn't take the pieces. He picks up his hat and starts toward the door; his face is set and masklike.

226. THE BEDROOM

Victoria lying back comfortably against the pillows of the bed. Into the mouthpiece she is reading the second of the two poems that she has spread out on her knees.

VICTORIA
> *(into phone, serious and absorbed)*
> "Be my wife in the strife for life
> In the hustle and bustle of everyday life,
> Be my wife, be my wife,
> Be my teeny weeny darling little wife,
> Be my little, little, little, little wife."
> *(pause)* ·
> *(she speaks doubtfully into the phone)*
> Are you still there?

BLURRED VOICE
> *(from receiver)*
> Y-e-e-es.

Wales comes in.

WALES
> I'll take it now, dear.

Victoria hands him the phone.

227. RITZ BAR—4:30 P.M.

CAMERA PANS through crowd, picking up a noisy party composed of Mr. Dorini, a New York bootleg chief, two friends, and a Fourth Man whose back is toward us. CAMERA PICKS UP PAUL, passing their table and PANS with him to DWIGHT SCHUYLER alone at a table against the wall.

152

PAUL
(to Schuyler, indicating Dorini)
I don't encourage that clientele.

He signals a waiter to clean up Schuyler's table.

PAUL
(half to himself)
Serving a bootlegger!
(as Schuyler looks up without much interest)
Sure! It's Dorini!

Schuyler looks at the other table.

SCHUYLER
(with recognition)
Oh, yes.

PAUL
(indignantly as he starts out of shot)
Killers!

A BAR-FLY'S VOICE
—Went off the thirtieth floor of his new building—
right down into Fifty-third Street.

Schuyler is looking o.s. toward Dorini's party with sudden new interest.

228. FULL SHOT—WALES'S SALON
Victoria is bent over her knitting in the dusk. She lays it down, looks at bedroom door, then gets up and goes to the window. She feels momentarily depressed and lonely. As she starts back to her chair, there is a knock at the anteroom door.

VICTORIA
Come in.

153

229. ANTEROOM DOOR

Julia Burns comes in. She pauses by the door, unable to see for a moment.

JULIA
>
> Well, Victoria!

230. BY THE WINDOW—VICTORIA

—overjoyed to see her. Julia comes into shot.

JULIA
>
> What a light to knit in!
> *(switches on a lamp)*
> Are you alone?

VICTORIA
>
> Daddy's working. You see, the whole nation is liquidating.

Julia doesn't quite understand.

VICTORIA
>
> *(nodding gravely)*
> The bottom's fallen out of the street—or something.

WALES'S VOICE
>
> Victoria!

231. THE BEDROOM DOOR

—now open. Wales is looking out, the receiver still at his ear.

VICTORIA'S VOICE
>
> Yes, Daddy.

She comes into shot.

WALES

> Hold this a minute, dear, while I get you some dinner.

VICTORIA

> *(nodding)*
> Will you ask Miss Burns to examine you?
> *(she takes phone)*

Wales smiles, goes out of shot.

VICTORIA

> *(into phone)*
> Well, let's see—over here we have a heroine named Joan of Arc who was burned at the stake a while ago —I mean a few hundred years ago—

232. WALES AND JULIA—PHONE IN SHOT

WALES

> When are you sailing?
> *(picks up phone)*
> Room service.
> *(to Julia)*
> Won't you have dinner with us?
> *(into phone)*
> I want to order something for a little girl—o-h-h, get her green vegetables: beans, peas, spinach, turnips, beets, squash—something for a little girl.

Wales hangs up. Julia has picked up the broken pieces of Schuyler's cane. She knows something has happened, and her face shows concern.

WALES

> I've got to go to America, too.

JULIA
> You'll take Victoria?

WALES
> Naturally.

A knock at the door.

WALES
> Come in.
> *(sees broken stick in Julia's hand)*
> Mr. Schuyler's property. While I was ill he was extremely busy.

Pageboy comes into shot with cable. Wales doesn't look at it yet. He tips Pageboy, who goes off.

WALES
> *(to Julia)*
> But at least I have a *little* left—and maybe in a week I can build it up to something.
> *(starts o.s.)*
> Please stay. Order dinner for yourself and me. I'll be through trading in half an hour.

CAMERA PANS with him, leaving Julia out of shot. He opens the cable, reads it, stops, crumples it, turns, comes back toward Julia, who is again in shot, taking off her hat. She looks up inquiringly.

WALES
> I'm through *now*. Schuyler didn't leave me anything.
> *(smiles wryly)*
> I was under the impression I had three hundred and fifty thousand in Liberty Bonds, but Mr. Schuyler got there first. I've been playing without a ball.
> *(pause)*
> Victoria and I are sailing for America tomorrow.

233. CLOSE SHOT—THE RITZ BAR—MR. DORINI AT HIS TABLE

DORINI
(talking off)
Dis is better'n what I handle in New York, Mr. Schuyler.
(laughs boisterously)

ANGLE WIDENS slightly to include Schuyler, who is putting all his resources into a genial smile.

DORINI
I like dis hotel. I like to move here. My hotel's full of foreigners. No real Americans.

234. NEARBY—PAUL
—passing the table with distaste. Seeing Schuyler with the gangsters, he reacts with surprise. CAMERA PANS OFF Paul, picking up in turn Schuyler, Dorini, two of his friends, and then CLOSING UP SWIFTLY on the man whose back has been toward us. It is the YOUTH IN THE CLOSE-FITTING TOPCOAT, whom we should recognize from Sequence A. (Suggest casting the "Sniper" from *Three Comrades*)

DISSOLVE TO:

235. CLOSE SHOT—WALES'S SALON—SEVEN O'CLOCK— VICTORIA FINISHING DINNER

VICTORIA
(counting metal covers)
Nine vegetables! Daddy!

CAMERA PULLS BACK to include Julia at table. Wales, who has left his place to get a cigarette, is in b.g. Waiter comes into shot, setting cake on table.

VICTORIA
     Cake, Daddy?

236. CLOSE SHOT—WALES

WALES
     No, thanks.

Wales brushes his hand over his eyes. Now we hear, as if far away, the sound of a ticker—*clack, clack, clack-clack, clack, clack*—then fainter voices, half a dozen of them:

          —U.S. Steel down ten.
          —Union Carbide down five.
          —Dodge Motors average.
          —Rails up.
          —Radio up three, bears move to cover.
          —Market holds. Steady trading.
          —Three million shares by five o'clock.

He tosses his head as if to shake it off.

237. BY THE ANTEROOM DOOR
Marion coming in with the lawyer we saw in Sequence C. CAMERA PANS with them up to table. Marion's eyes are blazing.

WALES'S VOICE
     Hello, Marion. Just in time for some birthday cake.

He comes into shot and turns to lawyer, expecting an introduction—the face is vaguely familiar.

LAWYER
     We've met before, Monsieur Wales.

MARION
               (*choking with anger*)
     This is Mr. Silve, Charles, the lawyer who drew up the guardianship papers.

158

WALES
> *(now on his guard)*
> Oh, yes. I was a pretty sick man, then. Thanks to
> Miss Burns here, I'm a great deal better.

MARION
> Are you all right, Victoria?

VICTORIA
> Naturally, Aunt Marion. I've been helping Daddy
> play the market on the phone.

MARION
> Put on your hat, dear.

Victoria looks at her father, but Wales is looking at Marion.
Victoria goes out of shot. Julia starts to follow.

MARION
> Don't go, please, Miss Burns!
> *(tensely to Wales)*
> Do you realize that bringing Victoria here is kidnap-
> ping under French law?

Wales's face protests.

LAWYER
> She is right, Monsieur.

WALES
> *(impatient)*
> Marion, I'm taking Victoria to America and that'll
> save you any more of this silly fretting.

MARION
> You're *not* taking Victoria to America. Till she's eigh-
> teen, she belongs to me, and all your money can't
> change it.

WALES
> *(gently)*
> I haven't got any money, Marion.

238. BY THE WINDOW—VICTORIA
She has her hat and bag and is leaving her poems on the table. She sees Schuyler's broken cane and can't resist the temptation of putting it together.

239. GROUP SHOT—THE OTHERS

MARION
> *(her voice low and full of hatred)*
> You've got to understand that this is the end. You've spoiled one life and you can't spoil another. I don't care about your dirty gambling, whether you make money or lose it. I don't want it for the child. Stick to your women who will have you.
> *(her eyes flicker momentarily toward Julia,*
> *then to the bottle on the table)*
> —And your drink and your luxury.

WALES
> *(deliberately)*
> Oh, bananas!

240. ANOTHER ANGLE
—showing Victoria reapproaching in b.g. Julia warns Wales with a head shake to be careful.

LAWYER
> Madame Petrie can call in the police, Monsieur. To change the settlement you would have to go to the courts—you would find it a difficult and expensive matter.

CAMERA FAVORS WALES. He sees at last that he is losing Victoria. Victoria comes into shot.

VICTORIA
>> *(to her father)*
>> When are we sailing?

WALES
>> *(sharply)*
>> Marion—

JULIA
>> *(interrupts by speaking to Victoria)*
>> Dear, go along with your aunt tonight. Your father needs rest.

At this assumption of authority, Marion turns angrily to Julia.

MARION
>> *(with irony)*
>> Ah, the maternal instinct!
>> *(overdoing it)*
>> You should have a husband and child of your own.

JULIA
>> I had a husband and a child, Madame Petrie. I lost them a year ago.

Marion is subdued by this statement—which was Julia's intention in making it. CAMERA FAVORS VICTORIA and JULIA, Victoria pressing Julia's hand. The Lawyer indicates to Marion to take Victoria and go. Victoria looks at her father. He nods.

VICTORIA
>> *(in a flat voice)*
>> It's always that.

Marion takes Victoria's hand.

VICTORIA
>（looking at her father with infinite reproach）
>You wouldn't go without me?

No answer. She turns and goes with Marion toward the door. Lawyer remains in shot handing Wales a card.

LAWYER
>（in a low voice）
>If you decide on the courts, Monsieur, I can recommend this lawyer.

He goes out.

JULIA
>（gently to Wales）
>Thank you. Victoria mustn't be let in for anything more.

He nods in agreement.

WALES
>They've done these things while I was asleep, but I'm awake now.

JULIA
>Are you going to America without her?

WALES
>I don't dare. I'd lose her—they'd take her like they're taking my good name. I've got to find some man here who believes in me.
>（thoughtfully）
>There's one chance—Van Greff in Switzerland. Will you see if there's a plane tonight?

As Julia picks up the phone—the *sound of an airplane motor begins o.s. and the scene—*

DISSOLVES TO:

162

SEQUENCE E

FADE IN:

241. AIRPLANE SHOT OF A CORNER OF LAKE GENEVA
—the hills rising from the Lake.

DISSOLVE TO:

242. SHOT ESTABLISHING HAUTEMONT
—which is on a peak and consists only of the GRAND HOTEL, a small hotel and the various grounds, tennis courts, etc., pertaining to them.

243. INT. UPPER CORRIDOR OF GRAND HOTEL
—Bellboy with note on salver knocking at a door. Valet opening it.

BELLBOY
     For Mr. Van Greff.

244. LIVING ROOM OF A LARGE SUITE—OLD MR.
     VAN GREFF
—sitting, his two canes near him. Beside him his English secretary in a morning coat with cables in his hand. Valet comes into shot with note that the secretary opens.

SECRETARY
                    (reading the note)
          Again!
                    (to Van Greff as valet goes out)
          Do you know a Mr. Wales?

VAN GREFF
                    (with interest)
          Charles Wales? Certainly. There's a young man!

SECRETARY
          Oh, I didn't realize—

VAN GREFF
                    (interrupting)
          What does he want?
                    (he takes the note)

245. FULL SHOT—OUTDOOR TERRACE OF THE HOTEL
—bounded by a circular walk. Back of the walk are tables
under big umbrellas. It is six o'clock and many people are
still at tea on the cliff high above the lake. An orchestra is
playing "Tiptoe Through the Tulips."
246. SECTION OF THE CIRCULAR WALK
—edged with a rail where the cliff falls sheer several hundred feet. We pick up the solitary figure of Charles Wales
walking along and stopping to look out over the scene
below. We do not see his face until Van Greff's Secretary,
accompanied by a Bellboy, comes into Shot. Bellboy indicates Wales and goes out of scene.

SECRETARY
          Mr. Charles Wales?

Wales turns—nods.

SECRETARY
>Mr. Wales, Mr. Van Greff would be pleased if you
>would dine with him tonight.

WALES
>*(gravely)*
>Thank you. How is Mr. Van Greff?

SECRETARY
>He holds his own very well.

They both look out at the view over the rail.

247. PROGRESS SHOT
—showing the car of the Funicular (mountain railway)
climbing slowly up the hill.

NOTE: a funicular consists of two parallel tracks built on a
mountain side at an angle of anywhere from fifty to ninety
degrees. There are two cars, connected by a cable that
passes around a wheel at the top.

SECRETARY'S VOICE
>*(over shot)*
>That car will take on water at the top and pull the
>*other* one up.

WALES
>*(nodding)*
>I wonder who thought of it first.

248. CLOSE SHOT—THE SLANTING CAR CLIMBING

249. INT. CAR—CLOSE SHOT VICTORIA
The car is open like an old-fashioned trolley. Long-
stemmed flowers dangle in and Victoria picks one quickly
en route. She looks up and o.s.

250. VIEW OF THE HOTEL FROM BELOW
Very close now. The circular walk plainly visible.

251. INT. CAR—VICTORIA

CAMERA MOVES OFF HER to show the YOUTH IN THE CLOSE-FITTING TOPCOAT in a back seat of the Funicular.

DISSOLVE TO:

252. LOBBY OF THE HOTEL—VICTORIA BY THE DESK

VICTORIA
(to clerk)
Thank you. I'm his daughter.

As she turns away from desk, CAMERA PANNING WITH HER, the Youth comes into shot as if casually. He walks along beside her, CAMERA TRUCKING IN FRONT OF THEM.

YOUTH
(to Victoria)
Mr. Wales your father?

VICTORIA
(not very pleased)
Yes.

He drops a little behind her; she is uncertain whether he wants to be led to her father or what.

253. EXT. TERRACE

Victoria and Youth coming out. Victoria looks around and sees her father out on the Walk. The Youth's eyes follow hers with interest. Victoria, followed by the Youth, starts off.

254. WALES AND VAN GREFF'S SECRETARY

SECRETARY
(cordially)
Seven thirty then. Good afternoon, Mr. Wales.

As he goes out of scene Wales looks off, and is astonished to see Victoria.

255. VICTORIA

—a little way off, running toward him full speed, CAMERA PANNING WITH HER. Wales takes her in his arms.

WALES

TOGETHER   Well, what the—

VICTORIA

Oh, I've got so much to—

VICTORIA

(remembering the Youth and turning)
Oh, there's a—

256. ANOTHER ANGLE—SHOWING THAT

—the Youth has disappeared

257. VICTORIA AND WALES

VICTORIA

Oh! there *was* a man who wanted to see you.

WALES

(lightly)
Undoubtedly the police. Darling, how did you know I was here?

VICTORIA

I called the Ritz early this morning.

WALES

(touched)
Were you worried?

VICTORIA

(smiles)
I was glad. It would have been harder to get to America with thirty francs.

WALES
　　　But how on earth did you *get* here? In a rocket?

VICTORIA
　　　Oh, Daddy, don't ask me now! Just let me *be* here for
　　　a minute, will you?
　　　(she looks around with a long sigh of appreciation)
　　　Now this is really the world of fashion, isn't it?

He smiles and takes her hand, turning to the rail.

WALES
　　　They come *here* to look down *there*. You can't get
　　　away from it no matter how high you climb.

VICTORIA
　　　I suppose it's very gay up here—fetes and galas.

WALES
　　　　　　　(nodding)
　　　There's probably a party this very night.

Victoria sighs.

WALES
　　　And I think we can go—after you tell me how you
　　　got here.

VICTORIA
　　　Well, it's really all due to some people who went
　　　jibber-jabber-jibber-jabber. You know that language?

WALES
　　　Oh yes.

VICTORIA
　　　　　　　(indicating her clothes)
　　　But Daddy, I'm practically—Cinderella.

WALES
> Those are grand clothes.

VICTORIA
> Not for parties.

DISSOLVE TO:
258. WALES'S ROOM—THE HOTEL HOUSEKEEPER
—a gray-haired Swiss. Beside her a chambermaid.

HOUSEKEEPER
> If you had told me, Mr. Wales, I could have sent
> down for a dress, but the last Funicular—

259. ANOTHER ANGLE—WALES
—sitting by the window (and establishing the window).
Victoria sits on the big bed.

WALES
> *(abandoning the idea)*
> Thanks anyhow.

WALES (cont.)
> *(to Victoria)*
> Well, darling, I'm dining with Mr. Van Greff—

260. ANOTHER ANGLE
The Housekeeper has started to turn away, but at the
sound of the name both she and the maid stiffen.

WALES (cont.)
> But afterwards I'll—

HOUSEKEEPER
> *(turning, her mouth half open)*
> Mr. Wales, I suppose if you *have* to have a dress—

MAID
>
> *(quickly and actively)*
> Perhaps we could borrow—

WALES
>
> *(mischievously, as if to Victoria)*
> I hear that Mr. Van Greff's lost everything—

Housekeeper and maid pause—as if on a stopped film.

WALES (cont.)
>
> —but it's not true.

They resume their flurry.

DISSOLVE TO:

261. VICTORIA'S ROOM
Smaller than her father's—single bed.
The Housekeeper is basting a white long formal organdy dress on her. A knock at the door and Wales puts his head in.

VICTORIA
>
> Daddy, listen!

WALES
>
> *(staring at her)*
> Good Heavens, I've lost you.

VICTORIA
>
> *(a little alarmed)*
> What do you mean?

WALES
>
> *(repeating thoughtfully)*
> I've lost you.

VICTORIA

    Oh no!—Oh you mean—
        (she touches the dress)
    Daddy, will you look over at me sometimes while
    you're having dinner—or wouldn't that be polite?
    Shall I sit where I can see the back of you or the
    front—or the sideways.

262. SECTION OF THE GRAND DINING ROOM DOWNSTAIRS

Victoria choosing a side table where a Waiter has just escorted her.

WAITER

    Here, Mademoiselle?

Victoria nods. Waiter hands her menu. Victoria tries to look around the Waiter's body on both sides to see if her father has arrived.

WAITER

    Some vegetables, Mademoiselle.

VICTORIA

        (resentfully)
    Vegetables!

WAITER

    Petit pois, pommes de terre—

On Victoria's face an expression of horror.

263. MEDIUM SHOT—DOOR OF THE DINING ROOM

Wales coming in, looking around. Head waiter approaches.

WALES
        Mr. Van Greff's table.

HEAD WAITER
                (impressed)
        Monsieur Van Greff is not down yet.

CAMERA TRUCKS IN FRONT OF THEM through the crowd. Wales
sees Victoria, smiles.
264. VICTORIA AND WAITER
He is tapping rather impatiently on his card, but he has
moved aside, so Victoria smiles at her father.

VICTORIA
                (explaining)
        That's a relation of mine. Bring me *poulet à la reine*.

WAITER
                (pointing to the card)
        Perhaps with some—

VICTORIA
        No vegetables!

Waiter's mouth protests—but Victoria looks at him so in-
tently that he withdraws.
265. WALES AND HEAD WAITER
—reaching a large window table for two about forty feet
from Victoria. Head Waiter pulls out the chair.

WALES
        Thank you.
                (he looks o.s., sees Victoria)

266. VICTORIA
—smiling. Her smile fades but she continues to look at
him affectionately. She points one finger down, indicating
for him to sit.

172

267. VAN GREFF'S TABLE

Wales gestures to indicate that the table is empty. He continues to look at her and evidently she signals to sit down anyway, so obediently he does so. Then he looks again at her, waiting instructions.

268. VICTORIA

She goes through the motion of lighting a cigarette, points at him to indicate he should do so.

269. VAN GREFF'S TABLE

Wales has not understood the pantomime. He puzzles a minute, then he takes a pencil out of his pocket, puts it in his mouth, and looks at her questioningly.

270. VICTORIA

She shakes her head and gives an elaborate demonstration of smoking in which she almost but not quite tips over a water glass.

271. VAN GREFF'S TABLE

Wales understands, takes out a cigarette, and lights it. He looks over at her questioningly.

272. VICTORIA'S TABLE

She nods.

273. MED. SHOT—THE ORCHESTRA

—tuning up.

274. VAN GREFF'S TABLE

A soft waltz has begun l.s. Mr. Van Greff's secretary comes into the Shot beside Wales. There is shock and grief in his face.

SECRETARY
    Mr. Wales.

WALES
    Yes?

                    (recognizing him)
    Oh yes.

173

SECRETARY

> Mr. Van Greff left us very suddenly fifteen minutes ago.

WALES

> *(shocked)*
>
> Oh.

SECRETARY

> It came very quickly. He had no pain.

WALES

> *(stands up)*
>
> Oh, I'm so terribly sorry.

SECRETARY

> He had spoken of you so pleasantly only a little before.

WALES

> So very sorry.

SECRETARY

> *(he is slowly withdrawing)*
>
> I have many messages to send.

275. VICTORIA'S TABLE

The waiter is serving her first course and again she is shifting her head a little to see her father.

276. VAN GREFF'S TABLE

Wales stands for a moment in thought then sits down, staring. This of course has had the double effect on him of natural shock and of the withdrawal of his last great hope. A Waiter comes into Shot.

WAITER

> Mr. Van Greff will not be dining?

WALES
    What? No.

He comes to himself, looks at Victoria

277. VICTORIA

—watching the orchestra, her feet beating time under the table. She looks at her father, smiles.

278. WALES

He smiles too.

279. VICTORIA

She points at the orchestra.

280. WALES

He nods, takes out his pencil, writes a note on a piece of paper, folds a bill into it, beckons o.s. Waiter comes into Shot.

WALES
    Ask the orchestra to play this tune when the dancing
    starts.

He gets up and starts toward Victoria.

281. VICTORIA

—looking o.s. surprised as Wales comes into Shot.

VICTORIA
    Isn't your friend coming?

WALES
    No. My friend isn't coming tonight.

VICTORIA
    Well, of course I'm sorry, but of course I'm really
    glad.

He sits down. He is not going to let his troubles touch her tonight.

282. LOBBY OF THE HOTEL

CAMERA MOVES UP to a door beside which is a plaque:

LINNET, KAMMER AND STRAW

Members N.Y. Stock Exchange
Transactions de Bourse

283. INT. BROKERAGE OFFICE

Two dozen men and women in dinner clothes, very grave and concerned as they watch the falling market. One man is bent forward, his face on his hands, a woman keeps shaking her head as if to say "Oh, my God, my God, my God." A board boy erases the figure 102 and substitutes figure 89 opposite a stock, and a general whistle goes up. CAMERA PANS to the YOUTH standing by the door. He wears a dinner coat and smokes a cigar as he watches the board, but his face is lost in some dream of his own. His eyes go upward to a

284. CLOCK—STANDING AT NINE O'CLOCK

285. TIME DISSOLVE OF ONE HOUR

286. FULL SHOT—THE DINING ROOM

Soft lights, not too spectacular, playing on the dancers. It wouldn't be elaborate up in the mountains. The CAMERA PANS a little way into the crowd as if searching for Victoria and her father.

287. VICTORIA'S TABLE

Wales and Victoria. Wales smoking a cigarette.

WALES

> Darling, don't you think we'd better dance while they're playing your tune?

VICTORIA

> *(with reluctance; she is suddenly shy)*
> Well—if you think it's all right.

They stand up. The tune is "I'm Dancing with Tears in my Eyes." As they are about to start off, a couple stop dancing

176

a few feet away. The man and woman, both a little tight, come up to them.

MAN

Well, Charlie Wales! Certainly am glad to see you, old boy.

The girl throws her arms around Wales.

GIRL

Charlie, you darling. Imagine meeting—

Wales is polite, but it is apparent that this is a most unwelcome meeting.

GIRL

You've owed me a dance for ten years.

The man has stooped over Victoria. She looks at him noncommittally, but we know she's not pleased.

MAN

Well, you beau-u-u-tiful l'il half pint! You're going to knock the boys cold in a few years.

He seizes Victoria's hand and does a few steps in place, in which Victoria doesn't join, as she looks despairingly at her father. Her father takes the woman's hands, which are spread for dancing, and presses them gently, firmly together.

WALES

Cornelia, I can't dance with you now.

CORNELIA

(remembering his bereavement)
Oh, of course. Helen—

He shakes his head at her quickly, as if to say, "Be quiet."

CORNELIA
(*stupidly continuing*)
I'm so sorry, Charles. But I thought you were dancing with your daughter.

WALES
I am.

Wales goes to Victoria and takes her politely away from
the man.

WALES
Sorry, Tom.

He dances off with Victoria, CAMERA REMAINING on Tom and
Cornelia, who feel snubbed.
288. A LITTLE FARTHER OFF
Wales and Victoria dancing. Victoria looks up at him.

VICTORIA
(*gravely*)
It looks as if nobody wants us to have fun together,
doesn't it, Daddy?

Wales concentrates on making her have a good time.

WALES
Those people are just lonesome, honey.
(*in tones of pathos*)
They haven't found any-body to annoy *all-l-l* day.

She looks at him, takes her cue, and laughs.

WALES
So they had to annoy *some*body—just to practice.

VICTORIA
>Who are they?

WALES
>*(in a stage whisper)*
>Parasites.

VICTORIA
>From Paris?

WALES
>No, a parasite is something you find everywhere.
>*(whispers again)*
>They want something you've got.

VICTORIA
>What do they want?

WALES
>Sometimes it's your happiness.

VICTORIA
>*(looks around with interest)*
>How do they get to be that?

WALES
>Oh, they begin by not doing their lessons.

VICTORIA
>*(with a sigh)*
>I knew there'd be a moral in it.
>*(pause)*
>I wish there was some person who could talk to you
>without always ending up with a moral.

WALES
>Darling, from now on, word of honor, that'll be me.

They dance in silence a moment.

VICTORIA

    I suppose this is the happiest that you can ever get, isn't it?

WALES

    I suppose so. Just about.

VICTORIA

    (sorry for everybody else)
    I hope those parasites have found somebody to annoy, because they might as well be happy, too.

DISSOLVE TO:

289. BAR IN THE CORNER OF THE ROOM
—on high stools having lemonades.

WALES

    Of course, tonight's an exception. We've got to lead a regular life.
    (lightly)
    We've lost all our money and I've got to make some more.

VICTORIA

    (anxious)
    Will it be that I don't see you?
    (pause)

WALES

    Not if I can help it.

VICTORIA

    (sensitive to his tone)
    Well, if you can't we've been to this ball together, haven't we? And we went to tea that afternoon in

Paris. And the two days on the ship, do you remember the games we played? I mean, I can make up a whole day with you now—for the morning I could think we were playing games and talking like we did on the ship, and for the afternoon I can remember how that ice cream tasted with the whipped cream on it, and for the evening—oh, how we got away from the parasites—and this dress. So that makes a whole day, doesn't it, Daddy? So I could just think of it, over and over.

WALES
    Shall we dance?

DISSOLVE TO:

290. BY THE DOOR OF THE BALLROOM
Victoria and her father walking out. Her arm is through his and her head almost touching his sleeve.

VICTORIA
    I wasn't *really* asleep during that dance, Daddy. I may have *looked* asleep.

Wales smiles and slips his arm from hers and around her waist as they pass into the lobby.

A Bellboy comes into Shot.

BELLBOY
    Mr. Wales? . . . Mrs. Marion Petrie calling you from Paris.

Victoria comes wide awake and looks stricken.

WALES
    (handing him some change)
    Tell the operator that my daughter and I have gone mountain climbing.

BELLBOY
 Oui, Monsieur.

He goes out of shot. Wales and Victoria continue on, CAMERA TRUCKING before them.

VICTORIA
 I saw Mr. Schuyler in the station in Paris.

WALES
 (absently)
 Did you?

VICTORIA
 He's *my* parasite. The day he made Uncle Pierre sign that paper, he offered me ice cream—

Wales's face changes. He stops in his tracks.

WALES
 What paper?

VICTORIA
 (innocently)
 The paper he didn't want Aunt Marion to see.

WALES
 Did your Uncle Pierre sign it?
 (with mounting excitement, he calls o.s.)
 Oh, chasseur!
 (suddenly he bends over Victoria)
 Dear, did the paper have something to do with you?

VICTORIA
 (ruefully)
 Yes. Lately *everything* seems to have—

Wales stands up. CAMERA FAVORS HIS FACE. There is a light breaking over it now.

WALES
> *(to himself)*
By heaven, that is conspiracy. And now I've got Mr. Schuyler in my pocket!

A Bellboy comes into Shot.

WALES
I want Mr. Pierre Petrie in Paris.
> *(to Victoria)*
I'll be upstairs in five minutes.

291. TELEPHONE OPERATOR

OPERATOR
M. Wales voudrait parler à *Monsieur* Pierre Petrie.

DISSOLVE TO:

292. VICTORIA'S BEDROOM
She is in a borrowed dressing gown, folding up the white dress. With a knock, Wales comes in.

VICTORIA
What did Aunt Marion say?

Wales smiles.

WALES
I did all the talking.

VICTORIA
Good.

WALES
    I said I *might* let you visit her two weeks next summer—*if* we come to Europe.

He takes her in his arms.

WALES
    Darling, I suppose this is as happy as you ever get.

DISSOLVE TO:

293. WALES'S ROOM
A dim light burning. Wales comes in, his face shining. He goes toward the window. Out of the shadow behind him steps the YOUTH, a gun in his hand. Wales turns.

YOUTH
    Start walking backward.

He advances toward Wales, who retreats back toward window. The iron trelliswork on the open window is about hip high, so that if he continues he will go out. He stops, pressed against the sill.

YOUTH
    It don't matter to me whether you go out with a slug in you or not. If it's the slug, I throw the gun after you, that's all.

WALES
    Give me a minute, will you? I suppose this is Mr. Schuyler's theory that dead I'm still worth a million dollars.

YOUTH
            (impatiently)
    I've counted *one*.

Wales puts his foot on the windowsill, as if considering between the two.

WALES

It's a magnificent height to fall from—right in the current style. The higher you go the farther you drop.

YOUTH

I've counted two.

Suddenly one foot from the gunman's ear, the telephone shrills. Involuntarily he starts and takes his eyes off Wales for half a moment. In that split second, Wales strikes, knocking him against the corner of a wardrobe. The Youth is out—Wales picks up the gun from the floor. As he stands there panting, the phone rings again. Wales takes it up.

WALES

Hello . . . hello, dear . . .
(heartily)
I'm so glad you called that I can't tell you.

294. VICTORIA'S ROOM

Victoria sits sleepily on the bed, her dress beside her.

VICTORIA

I just wanted to know if I can keep the dress. I don't want to be extravagant, now we're out of Wall Street.

295. WALES'S BEDROOM

WALES

(tenderly)
Ah, you can keep it, darling.

After a moment he hangs up, steps over the unconscious body of the gunman to the window, and takes a deep breath. Then he looks at the gunman.

WALES
> *(ironically)*
> My last contact with high finance.

The gunman stirs—he looks very young.

WALES
> Lie still, little boy. I don't suppose your mother
> brought you up for this.
> *(he looks out the window again)*
> You have to put a lot into a child.

Far below, the orchestra has begun to play the tune he and Victoria danced to. Wales speaks with quiet confidence.

WALES
> Ah, there's a lot to live for.

The CAMERA MOVES to a CLOSE SHOT of him.

296. CLOSE SHOT—VICTORIA ASLEEP

By the single light still lit in her bedroom, we see that her expression is akin to his, as if in agreement with his sentiment. Sleep has overtaken her just before she managed to really get into bed. Still in her dressing gown, with one slipper off and one on, she lies across the bed with her new white dress clasped in her arms.

FADE OUT.

—THE END—

AFTERWORD

I saw that the novel, which at my maturity was the strongest and supplest medium for conveying thought and emotion from one human being to another, was becoming subordinated to a mechanical and communal art that, whether in the hands of Hollywood merchants or Russian idealists, was capable of reflecting only the tritest thought, the most obvious emotion. . . . there was a rankling indignity, that to me became almost an obsession, on seeing the power of the written word subordinated to another power, a more glittering, a grosser power. . . .

—F. Scott Fitzgerald

In *The Love of the Last Tycoon*, the Hollywood novel F. Scott Fitzgerald was writing at his death, this exchange occurs between the brilliant producer Monroe Stahr and the English novelist George Boxley:

> "I don't think you people read things. The men are duelling when the conversation takes place. At the end one of them falls into a well and has to be hauled up in a bucket."

"Would you write that in a book of your own, Mr. Boxley?"

"What? Naturally not."

"You'd consider it too cheap."

"Movie standards are different," said Boxley, hedging.

Since Fitzgerald wrote the screenplay for his story "Babylon Revisited" to support his work on *The Love of the Last Tycoon*, the pronouncements on the movies in the novel-in-progress bear on his practices as a screenwriter. He perforce set different standards for his movie work.

For the "Babylon Revisited" assignment Fitzgerald was required to enlarge a short story with very little action into a full-length screen drama by providing a new plot. Another Stahr instruction to Boxley is that "There's always some lousy condition" in movie-making. The lousy condition for the "Babylon Revisited" screenplay—that it was intended as a vehicle for Shirley Temple—necessitated that the child's role be augmented.

Fitzgerald's February 1931 *Saturday Evening Post* story occupies three days in Paris subsequent to the 1929 stock-market crash. It begins with Charlie Wales (Bonnie Prince Charlie? the Prince of Wales? Charlie Wails?) in the Ritz Bar, the epicenter of Babylonian dissipation for wealthy American expatriates during the twenties. He has returned to Paris to regain his daughter, Honoria, and the honor he sacrificed to alcoholic revelry during the boom. He is sober, solvent, and responsible. That evening Charlie visits Honoria; she is in the legal custody of his sister-in-law, who holds him responsible for his wife's death as the consequence of a drunken marital quarrel.

Charlie spends the next day with Honoria, encountering a pair of his erstwhile drinking companions. That evening Charlie obtains the promise of Honoria's return to him. On the evening of the third day of the story Charlie's discussion of arrangements with the sister-in-law is interrupted by the invasion of his uninvited drunken friends. These reminders of what Charlie had been deprive him of Honoria again. After returning to the Ritz Bar he ruminates on the distorting power of Paris in the twenties:

> —The men who locked their wives out in the snow, because the snow of twenty-nine wasn't real snow. If you didn't want it to be snow, you just paid some money.

The short story is encapsulated in these thirty-two words that bear the blindstamp of Fitzgerald and identify "Babylon Revisited" as his. (He is echoing *"Ou sont les neiges d'antan?"*) But there is no way to photograph these words: they do not appear in the screenplay.

In converting the material of the "Babylon Revisited" short story to images on the screen, Fitzgerald removed the *revisited* theme. Charlie does not return to Paris to recover his Honoria; in the screenplay Victoria seeks him out in Switzerland. Fitzgerald's own copy of his screenplay, dated August 1940, is titled *Cosmopolitan*—not an improvement in terms of appropriateness. It includes an "Author's Note":

> This is an attempt to tell a story from a child's point of view *without* sentimentality. Any attempt to heighten the sentiment of the early scenes by putting mawkish speeches into the mouth of characters—in short by doing what is locally known as "milking it," will damage the *force* of the piece. Had the present author intended, he could have broken down the sentimental section of the audience at many points, but the price would have been *the release of the audience too quickly from tension*—and one would wonder at the end where the idea had vanished—or indeed what idea had been purchased. So whoever deals with this script is implored to remember that it is *a dramatic piece*—not a homey family story. Above

all things, Victoria is a *child*—not Daddy's little helper who knows all the answers.

Another point: in the ordinary sense, this picture has no more moral than *Rebecca* or *The Shop Around the Corner*—though one can draw from it any moral one wishes about the life of the Wall Street rich of a decade ago. It had better follow the example of *Hamlet*, which has had a hundred morals read into it, all of them different—let it stand on its own bottom.

By all means—"let it stand on its own bottom."

—M. J. B.